BRKNVESSELS

&

KRAACKD

POTS

How to Surrender Your Will to Capture God's

Rene' Marie Jones

BRKNVESSELS & KRAACKD POTS

Copyright © 2019 by Rene' Marie Jones

Paperback ISBN: 978-0-578-45945-5

Cover Artwork: 99designs

All rights reserved. Printed in the United States. No part of this book may be reproduced, stored in a retrieval system, or transmitted in any form, or by any means, electronic, mechanical, photocopying, and recording in any manner without the written permission of the author.

All Scripture is taken from the New King James Version®. (NKJV) Copyright © 1982 by Thomas Nelson. Used by permission. Unless otherwise noted as New International Version (NIV)

For more information, contact
https://renemariejones.com
brknvessels@gmail.com

DEDICATION

This book is dedicated to several people. It is dedicated to those of you who are hungering and thirsting to know the reason and the "why" you were born. It is also for those of you who do not even know that there is a reason why there was a day, a month and a year divinely set aside on which you were born. Moreover, it is especially for those of you who are tired, weary and frustrated with fighting against and resisting destiny and you are now willing to wave the white flag of SURRENDER!

"And Mary said, 'Behold, I am the servant of the Lord; let it be to me according to your word.' And the angel departed from her."- Luke 1:38

ACKNOWLEDGEMENTS

The first person I must acknowledge is "ABBA", my heavenly Father, who knew me before I was formed in Joan's womb (my Mom). The second person is Jesus, who willingly left His place in heaven and came to this sin-sick planet to find and save me (from me) and from an eternal separation from my heavenly family. The third person is Holy Spirit. He is my Comforter, Friend, Teacher, Advocate, Helper, and He will quickly let me know when I am off course and heading for a life threatening and fatal collision.

Next, I acknowledge the leaders of my church who support me and the men, women, youth and children who embrace and allow me to humbly stand as their leader. Your lives, dreams, hurts, pains, struggles, victories and overcoming faith is the "stuff" that inspiration is made of. You have encouraged and pushed me to get "those books" out that were prophesied, and some even making sure I had enough journals to get started in (thanks, Regina ☺).

The man and the woman who "birthed" me in the spirit are Pastor Donald Q. Fozard and Elder Nora Fozard.

Thank you for laying down your lives for the people of God for His glory and honor. You showed me what true BRKNVESSELS are when I did not even know there was such a thing. In addition, you both taught me how to fight the good fight of faith, to persevere and never quit (and there were many times that I wanted to but did not dare entertain the thought for very long).

My Bible teacher, Elder Melvin Tolbert, instilled in me a love and passion for the Word of God. Thank you for stirring up the "gift" of teaching in me.

A heart of gratitude goes to my mother, Joan Randolph and her mother, my Nanny (I miss you still, Nanny. Thank you for praying for me and for Vacation Bible School summers). These two women took me and introduced me to the church and the reality that there is someone WHO is much BIGGER than I in control of EVERYTHING!

Thanks be to God for ALL the prayer warriors, contributors, counselors and advisors whose hands and hearts have touched this book. You thwarted the attempts of Satan's sabotage of this project and you kept me from tripping over my own feet!

Certainly not last and definitely not least, is the one who has walked, talked and lived as a BRKNVESSEL before my very eyes for the all the years that we have been husband and wife. He is a modern day example of what lives on the pages of the Bible. His unswerving trust, courage, humility and transparency breathes SURRENDER and FAITH in a God whose ways are not our ways and whose thoughts are not ours either.

Thank you, honey, for being my greatest cheerleader, encourager, critic, coach and friend. I would not and could not be who I am if it was not for you and God "teaming up" on me ☺. Love you!

Finally, I must acknowledge, the body of Christ. It is my desire that we become the bride, without spot or wrinkle, that Jesus Christ, our Husband, is coming for (Ephesians 5:27). It is my desire that we, as the sons and daughters of God, be revealed as a church that is deeply intimate, surrendered and totally sold out to God. It is then and only then, that it will be said of us as it was said of the early church, "these are they that have turned the world upside down" (Acts 17:6).

PREFACE

"For ALL have sinned and fall short of the glory of God"- Romans 3:23 (emphasis added).

Sin is a spiritually transmitted disease that was passed down through our spiritual ancestors, Adam & Eve (Romans 5:12-21). Every man, woman, boy and girl that's born into the world, will contract the sin "gene" and will be infected by this once "incurable" disease. Because of this disease, separation from God, brokenness, dysfunctionalism, sickness, poverty, and ultimately death is the lot of us all (Romans 6:23). However, thanks to God's love, grace and mercy, a "cure" was made available through the plan of salvation, the death, burial and resurrection of Jesus Christ, to anyone who believes and receives it (John 3:16-18). Salvation is the beautiful gift (Ephesians 2:8-9) that takes sinful and broken humanity from its mother's womb (Psalm 51:5), along with the fruit of brokenness that is produced throughout a life here on earth, into the promise of eternal life with the one who hung, bled and died for us, Jesus Christ ((Romans 6:23). We are made new (2 Corinthians 5:17) by God's Spirit and we are made whole and complete (Colossians 2:10).

Therefore, before we receive the gift of salvation, we come to God as "broken" vessels and dysfunctional, "cracked" pots. In its original context, "broken" and "cracked" portrays something that can be of little or no use, needing to be fixed. However, in order for God to use us for His glory and our intended purposes, we must be "brkn"! However, this time it is a graceful breaking by the hands of the Master Surgeon that He does to, through and in us so that we may be given out to be used by Him for His glory and honor. That is why I changed the spelling of "broken" (brkn) to have a different meaning and context in this book. In addition, with this context of usefulness for God's glory in mind, a "kraackd pot" has the potential of becoming useful as a brknvessel!

A BRKNVESSEL is one who is willing to totally and completely surrender their purposes, plans, and person to God to be BLESSED, BROKEN and GIVEN, as a vessel used for His glory and for His honor. Some have **CHOSEN** to be a brknvessel, infusing the world with the loving and fresh fragrance of the Lord. On the other hand, there are others who have **CHOSEN** to be kraackd pots, not willing to completely surrender or submit to the purposes that God has intended for their lives. Instead, they are limited in reach and impact in the kingdom of God because only small amounts of what is inside (heavenly treasure in earthen vessels) can seep out through the small cracks. SELF has not been BROKEN...yet!

I am excited about us starting our journey down the road towards the place of "brknness" in the hands of the Master! And I am confident and know that it is His desire to do and complete a great work in us because "we are his workmanship, created in Christ Jesus for good works, which God prepared beforehand, that we should walk in them" (Ephesians 2:10).

Blessings!
A BRKNVESSEL...no longer a KRAACKD POT

INTRODUCTION

All four Gospel accounts written by four different authors give us a bird's eye view of a "brknvessel". Jesus was taken and chosen by God to save humankind (Matthew 1:21), thanks was given for Him on the day He was born (Luke 2:8-14), His Father blessed Him (Matthew 3:17), He was broken (Isaiah 53:3-5, 7-12) and His life was given in exchange for ours (John 10:15-18). Finally, yet importantly, we have the record of the leading lady of Mark chapter fourteen. She cared not about the expense or sacrifice that her act would cost. Her breaking of the bottle was an outward manifestation of an inward broken spirit and contrite heart (Psalm 5:17). And the oil of her "brknness" still flows down to us today.

In Matthew 14:15-20 we have the account of Jesus feeding a mix multitude of 5,000 men, beside women and children. After having them all to be seated in groups, He took what was available, five loaves and two fish, from the hands of the disciples (as we were called out from the clutches of the world), gave thanks for it (for by grace were we thankfully saved), blessed it (blessed means holy and set apart), broke it (death to self and submitted to God) and gave it (a life that is in the service of the Most High God) to the people. The Bible tells us that not only were all filled but there were twelve baskets of broken pieces leftover, one for each apostle (that is my interpretation of it).

As we embark on our journey, we will look at HOW men and women in the Bible were "brkn" and how some were not willing to be so. You will also find out if you are a BRKNVESSEL or if you are a KRAACKD POT in need of further breaking in order to become a BRKNVESSEL! I pray that you will read over, meditate and put to heart the passages of Scripture we will share in this book. Also, my prayer is that you will surrender your will, mind and heart to God. I encourage you to pray and ask the Great Revelator and Illuminator Himself, Holy Spirit, to show you how to make His word come alive and bring about a suppleness and pliability to your vessel, to be molded and fashioned into what He wants. So, let's get started!

Contents

BRKNVESSELS i
& i
KRAACKD POTS i
DEDICATION iii
ACKNOWLEDGEMENTS iv
PREFACE vii
INTRODUCTION x
BRKNVESSELS & KRAACKD POTS 1
SWEET AND SOUR FAITH 4
BEING A FAILURE IS NOT AN OPTION 7
TEN TIMES BETTER 10
A ROSE BY ANY OTHER NAME 14
THE PEOPLE'S CHOICE 17
TAKE ANOTHER DIP 21
I'M TOO OLD TO HAVE A BABY 24
EVERYTHING THAT GLITTERS AIN'T GOLD 28
ANOTHER BAD HAIR DAY?! 32
JUST DO IT 37
WHEN THE ROOSTER CROWS 40
S.O.S. 44
RIPPLE EFFECT 47
THE MAT 51
FOOD FOR FISH 54
TO BE BORN OR NOT TO BE BORN 58
THE BLAME GAME 62
CRYING BABIES AND CROCODILES 65
START AT THE END 69
JOB SECURITY 73
NOW YOU SEE THEM, NOW YOU DON'T 77

GET YOUR HOUSE IN ORDER	81
THIS ISN'T BURGER KING!	84
POWER, PRESTIGE, POSITION	88
ONE LIFE TO LIVE	91
CRACKING UP	95
HIDDEN FAITH	99
LET GO OF THE BANANA	103
I HAVE A DREAM	106
WHO'S THE BOSS?	110
WHAT'S IN THAT LEADER?	114
SPOILED FRUIT	117
DID GOD REALLY MEAN IT?	121
FIVE THOUSAND PIECES AND MORE	126
SNOW WHITE	129
CALLED OUT OF TIME	134
CARS, HOUSES, AND BARNS	138
OIL FOR SALE	142
HOW ABOUT THOSE ANTS?	145
NETS AND FISHES	148
A MAN AND HIS BOAT	151
SKIN FOR SKIN	154
HE LOVES ME, HE LOVES ME NOT	157
A NEED TO KNOW BASIS	160
NOT FOR SALE	164
A MAN FOR ALL SEASONS	167
BIG I'S AND LITTLE YOU'S	171
ABOUT RENE'	174

BRKNVESSELS & KRAACKD POTS

Let us begin our journey by looking at two profiles, that of a young teenage girl who would have NEVER dreamed the impossible could happen and the other, an old man who dared to dream the IMPOSSIBLE but did not BELIEVE it when he was facing a dream come true.

Zacharias, a priest, was a highly respected man in his community, a leader in his church and the faithful and protective husband of a loving wife. Their long life together was full yet it was not complete. There had not been the sound of a baby's cry or the late night feedings and diaper changes. Now at this season in their lives, it was impossible (or was it?) to have children. Nevertheless, he dared to dream the impossible. One day as he was in the temple, he learned from an angelic visitation that his prayers had been heard and that he and his wife would be proud parents to a son name John. As the angel gave Zacharias the good news and shared the destiny and purpose of this son, doubt and unbelief began to swirl in his head. How can this be possible, an old man with an old and barren wife having a son? The angel's response to Zacharias was as a cold splash of divine water in his face. God sent the heavenly messenger with His word and truth. But because of DOUBT and UNBELIEF (James 1:6, Mark 16:14), the very thing that the hearer dared to once believe and even prayed from his own lips, will now shut those lips closed until the prophesy is fulfilled (Luke 1:20)

Six months later, another divine proclamation was announced to a young teen-age virgin who was engaged to be married. The angel told her that she would get pregnant and the child would be the Son of God. The thought would be a dream come true for a young, poor Jewish girl or any girl for that matter who was raised to believe the prophecies of a coming Messiah and desired that she would be the "favored" instrument that would make it possible. Unlike the angelic visit to Zechariah, this time the angel Gabriel met with a heart that not only believed the Word of God but dared to receive the Rhema (spoken word of God) which conceived in her womb, the living word of God (John 1:14).

So, what shut a mouth but opened a womb? Zechariah doubted the Word that was spoken to him because of his circumstances and the impossible situation that he was looking at. He could not believe that what was spoken could happen (Luke 1:18, 19). Sometimes, the very thing that we pray and believe God for in the beginning, wanes and waxes smaller and smaller in our hearts when the passing of the days, weeks, months and years loom larger and larger. Even when God sends a reminder and a confirmation of what we once believed, doubt and unbelief snuffs the light out. We "throw in the towel" even after we hear what is possible, no longer believing it to be so or the One who spoke it. Mary on the other hand chose to believe and receive the unbelievable. She questioned the "how" but she believed in the "WHO". Moreover, in spite of her circumstances, the possible loss of her husband-to-be, family, friends and even her very life, she chose ownership of the prophecy and claimed the promise of life in the face of potential death.

A brknvessel is a person who is willing to surrender EVERYTHING to God. No matter what their mind tells them (reasoning) or their emotions, their spirit will override. The more that we die to OUR selfish desires, OUR stubborn ways, even maybe OUR dreams, and letting go of any and every thing that would hinder our growth and relationship with God, we are "brkn". When God's way is not our way, His answer is "NO" and His timing is "not on time", we must decide to be still and trust that He knows what is best. His desire is that we TRUST and BELIEVE and be able to say as Mary did, "be it unto me according to your word, Lord" (Luke 1:38). This is the KEY to "brknness"! Any other response would just be kraackd pot gibberish.

Today, let your prayer be for the Holy Spirit to shine His light to reveal to you where you are in your trust and faith in God. I pray that you will be a willing vessel, submit, and place your heart in His loving hands!

SWEET AND SOUR FAITH

One can only imagine the devastation of being forced to leave familiar surroundings of home, with your husband and two sons, family and friends, because of an economic and financial crisis, move to a far country outside of your cultural and spiritual normalcy, and then the horror of losing your husband to death followed by your sons. What you are left with are mounting funeral costs, unpaid bills, no income, two daughters-in-law, and a heart that has been broken to match a faith that is now questionable. Naomi, whose name meant "pleasantness", changed it to Mara, which means "bitterness", "For the Almighty has dealt harshly with me. I went out full, and the Lord has brought me home again empty" (Ruth 1:20-21). A hardship and a severe crisis is where the harsh cold facts of reality will come face to face with who and what we say we believe in.

Naomi's daughter-in-law Orpah decided to return to the place from whence she came. We often will make the same choice when our dreams have been shattered and hope is replaced by despair and hopelessness. Ruth, whose name means, "vision" and "friend", on the other hand, chose to stay. Her pledge of loyalty and commitment to Naomi is the foundation of the marital covenant vows that have been exchanged between a husband and wife at the altar down through the ages,

"...For where you go, I will go, and wherever you lodge I will lodge. Your people shall be my people and your God my God... The Lord do so to me and more also, if anything but death parts you and me" (Ruth 1:16-17). She keeps her "vows" as they both return back to Bethlehem (house of bread) when news comes to them that the economic situation had changed for the better. So the table had turned. For Naomi, she was going back to a place of familiarity but Ruth would be an outsider, away from her home Moab, its culture, her family, and friends.

Ruth's "conversion" (1:16-18) and devotion to her mother-in-law (Ruth 2:10-11), proceeded her and was noised about in her new home (Ruth 2:5-7). Thus, when Naomi saw an opportunity for their redemption through the marriage of Ruth to a relative, she carefully instructed Ruth what to do to insure her future. Ruth submitted to the counsel that secured a place in the heart of the relative, Boaz. This godly, wealthy and influential man lived up to his name, swiftly setting in motion the process to buy back the name and family of his dead relatives through his marriage to Ruth as her kinsman redeemer.

Naomi and Ruth, were both, two women victimized by extreme loss, sorrow and grief. The one, who started out in faith, allowed her pain and despair to turn into "sour" unbelief and doubt, leaving a bitter taste in her mouth and heart. While the other chose to take the sour bitterness and sweeten it with hope and faith. Putting trust in a God that she came to know and love opened the door for her to have a place in the lineage of Jesus Christ (Matthew 1:1-6). Her son, Obed, whose name means "worship" was the grandfather of King David (Ruth 4:22).

We can be a KRAACKD POT that will only survive, going through the motions of life living with the limitations and restrictions of a painful past. Or, we can give the past to God, totally surrendering to His plan and will for our lives, no matter how painful, trusting His heart when we cannot see His hand. If so, we will sing a song of worship, the song of a BRKNVESSEL....

"Worship is the sun bursting through the last of the darkened storm clouds, drying up the flood waters that sought to take you down for the third time. It is the sword that cuts away the ropes of despair and discouragement that seem to squeeze the very life out of you. It is the song that escapes from a dry and parched throat, made so by the cries of despondency and frustration, asking, "WHY?" It is a soothing and healing balm placed on an open and bleeding wound, inflicted by the knife of a loved one or those who said, 'I would never hurt or leave you'. It is the garment of dignity that clothes you after you have been stripped naked and raped by those closest to and trusted by you. It is the restorer of life when they thought they had killed you and left you for dead. It is the means whereby you will soar with the wings of an eagle, walk and not faint, run and not be weary, and STRENGTH, FAITH and HOPE is renewed again".

BEING A FAILURE IS NOT AN OPTION

The children of Israel of Moses' day were challenged daily to trust God when they left Egypt, along with a mixed multitude of slaves. It was during their journey from Egypt to Mount Sinai that God began to transform them from descendants of 400 years of slavery to His people. However, what should have only taken them eleven days took 40 long years. Our study today in 1 Corinthians 10:1-13, recaps their "failures" and the reasons why God took them for a scenic trek through the wilderness of Sinai (Numbers 32:13).

Moses was God's chosen leader and deliverer for Israel. He led them, fed them, taught them, protected and interceded for them. Even though this great multitude of 2 million plus people all received the same from their leader, "nevertheless, God was not pleased with most of them; their bodies were scattered in the wilderness" (1 Corinthians 10:5). The Israelites carried the practice of idolatry out of Egypt with them. It was not long after crossing the Red Sea and at the foot of Mount Sinai where

Moses had been 40 days with the Lord that they used the natural elements of gold and made another god, a golden calf, to lead them since their leader was MIA (missing in action). When we take our eyes off the true and living God, we will make gods out of our children, mates, careers, fortunes and our achievements.

Sexual immorality is blatant in our society today but it is not new. While in Shittim, the Israelite men (most of whom were leaders) took the Moabite women as wives, all proudly and unashamedly in the face of Moses and God. These forbidden and unholy alliances led them into idol worship and all of the sexual practices that go along with bowing down to and serving the Moabite idols of lust and fertility. Twenty-four thousand people lost their lives in a plague that God sent (Numbers 25:1-16). As people of God, we must be careful whom we associate ourselves with. Evil communications and relationships do corrupt our spiritual lives and ultimately our relationship with God.

The children of Israel became impatient enroute from Mount Hor to the Red Sea, complaining and murmuring against Moses and God. Therefore, God sent venomous snakes that bit and killed many until the very man that they murmured against had to pray to God for their deliverance. Impatience can cause us to make decisions and do things that we would not ordinarily. God's timing is never late or early but always on time. We must be careful how we treat the men and women who represent God- "touch not my anointed and do my prophet no harm" (Psalm 105:15) God tells us.

There were many failures of the Moses generation of the children of Israel (Kraackd pots). Nevertheless, God raised up a generation from among them who learned from those failures. They followed, obeyed and accomplished His purpose of conquering and possessing the Promised Land under the leadership of Joshua.

Sometimes we may and will miss the mark and have failures as we follow God. However, we can look at the examples and experiences of those who have come and gone before us, to know what to do and what not to do. Let us follow them as they followed God. Know for certainty that you too may fail but you are NOT a failure.

TEN TIMES BETTER

Imagine being chosen by the President to be trained and on his staff to help with the leadership of this country. As part of the training and preparation for this high and sought after honor, you were given a new name that was more fitting for the protocol of the White House, a new wardrobe to replace the modest one you had, and a new diet of food and drink that only White House officials could partake of. Sounds good? Yes, maybe, but there is a hiccup. The changing of a name is not really an issue. Neither was the changing of clothes to fit the culture of the greatest house in this country. However, what about the partaking of food that is forbidden by your faith and your God?

Four young Hebrew boys were deported from their homes and taken captive along with the rest of their people to Babylon, the foreign land of their captors. They were assigned to an official of the court whose three-year responsibility was to teach them the language, literature, culture and religion of their new home and position (Daniel 1:3-5). The Babylonians worshipped many gods; Anu, the sky god, Ea, god of fresh water, known for his wisdom, Ishtar (root word of Easter), goddess of love, fertility, and war, Sin, god of the moon, and Shamash, god of the sun and of justice, to name a few. In acts of worship and paying tribute to these gods, food was offered as a sacrifice to them and then eaten by the worshippers. In many cultures today, for special occasions, family and social gatherings, food is often the centerpiece that binds the gatherers together. With the knowledge of what happened to the food before it came to their table, the young men declined from partaking of it. Instead, they had their own simple and plain menu. It was a menu that was to be tested out on them for ten days by the official assigned to them. They promised him that instead of them faring less than the other young men who were eating at the king's table, they would fare better. The official agreed but only after being assured by Daniel that he would not get in trouble with the king, risking the loss of his head. (Daniel 1:11-14).

At the end of ten days, not only did the young Hebrew men look better, they were healthier and more nourished than the other youth who ate the prescribed food commanded by the king. Three years later, when the training was over, the chief official presented his wards to the king. His young protégés were more skilled than the other young men and "in every matter of wisdom and understanding about which the king questioned them, he found them ten times better than all the magicians and enchanters in his whole kingdom" (Daniel 1:20).

Ten times better! Daniel and his three friends refused to compromise their character, integrity, their faith or their God. They were willing to stand on the Solid Rock and trust Him with the results. What were those results? In spite of the meager and plain diet they chose to eat, they were healthier than the others who ate what the king offered. The world does seem to have a fancier and more appetizing menu from which to choose from, otherwise there would be no temptation to make a choice. Television, movies and the media presents its dainties of designer clothing, cars, music, glamorous men, women, and money on the platters of the world. Now there is nothing wrong with any of these things unless you trade your soul, literally, to gain them and will do anything to keep and obtain more of them (Mark 8:36). Man shall not live by only the natural bread that he eats but by the words that come from God's mouth and are penned in His book, the Bible. Those words are health to the bones and life to the flesh (Proverbs 4:20-22).

God rewarded these young men with wisdom and knowledge beyond their years and natural intellect. The wisdom of God is higher than and not to be compared with that of man's (1 Corinthians 1:20-25). The fear of God is the beginning of wisdom and if we lack it, it is ours for the asking. Daniel and his friends were promoted and given high positions in the king's court as advisors. God blessed Daniel with the special gift of the interpretation of dreams. Living a long and productive life, this young man counseled and interpreted dreams for three heathen monarchs during the 70-year long captivity of Israel in a foreign land.

The church is not and does not have to be in competition with the world. We are called out to be separate and there should be a distinction between God's people and the people of the world. Compromising godly standards and principles can be a deadly trap for the child of God. However, standing firm on His word not only will bring His rewards, it is TEN TIMES BETTER!

A ROSE BY ANY OTHER NAME

"A rose by any other name would smell as sweet" is a frequently quoted line from William Shakespeare's play Romeo and Juliet. Juliet's lover, Romeo, is from her family's rival, the house of Montague. The quote implies that a name does not necessarily define who or what we are.

As 1 Chronicles chapter 4 opens, we see the lineage of the tribe of Judah. Judah was the fourth born son of Jacob (who was later named Israel by God) and Leah, his first wife. Each tribe is influential in the nation of Israel and has the honor of being descended from the Jews' ancestor, Jacob, but the tribe of Judah was given prominence, power and praise. It is from this tribe that most of Israel's kings descended. Even though Judah was not the oldest son of Jacob, God's selection of him and his descendants to sit upon the throne of Israel demonstrated God's sovereignty and divine purposes for His people even when tradition and convention are contrary to His ways.

The first eight verses of First Chronicles opens with a list of families, specifically the fathers, the wives, and the names of their sons and daughters. However, when we get to verse nine, no such details are given. Unlike the family tree's names prior to this, there is no mention of Jabez's mother's name, names of his siblings or any mention of his father at all. His name meant "pain" and this label was the one his mother gave him because of her experience birthing him into the world. The world will often put labels on its children, "stupid", "slow", a "bad boy", a "fast girl". Contrary to the old nursery rhyme that says "sticks and stones may break my bones, but words will never hurt me", words, labels and the wrong names can and do hurt. The stigma of walking around being called "Pain" as the result of someone else's experience could have damaged and destroyed Jabez. However, his "brknness" led him instead to the One who has a name above every name.

Jabez's prayer has been known as "The Prayer of Jabez" and it came from a heart that was surrendered to God. The first thing that he prayed for was God's blessing, "oh, that you would bless me indeed". He knew that what God blessed, no man could curse regardless of what name he called you or label he ascribes to you. God knows your name and calls you by one that no man knows. A second aspect of that blessing would be the "enlarging of my territory". Your territories are the areas in which God has you in, your job, community, school, your family and walk in life. God wants to give us influence in these areas so that we will make and have an impact for His glory. Next, his request was that "your hand would be with me". We cannot do anything and be a success in this life without the power of God. When His hand is upon us, all things are possible. His hand will guide and lead us in the directions that we need to go in. The enemy of our soul, Satan, is ever lurking around us, seeking to devour us and to steal, kill and destroy the plans and purposes of God for our lives. We are not to be ignorant of the tactics he uses but we are to ask God to "keep us from evil". The last part of this powerful prayer is "that I may not cause pain". Jabez remembered daily the pain that his birth caused his mother. Every time his name was called, "Pain", he experienced himself the pain of it all. When you have been hurt and have lived with pain, you are sensitive to the pain and hurt of others. It was not his desire to be the cause of anyone's hurt or disappointments.

Before we end our story of Jabez, we must note something that is very important. Verse 9 says, "Now Jabez was more honorable than his brothers..." It is irrelevant that we do not know their names. All that we need to know is that "a good name is to be chosen rather than great riches, and favor is better than silver or gold" (Proverbs 22:1). Jabez may not have had a good name chosen for him but he had something better. He had the favor of God. We know that God held him in His arms and did not see him as the name he was called. In fact, to the Lord, it did not matter what they called him. The end of verse 10 tells us "God granted him what he requested". God heard his prayer and answered it. That's the F-A-V-O-R of God upon a BRKNVESSEL!

THE PEOPLE'S CHOICE

Imagine being invited to the home of one of the most revered and powerful preachers in America. As you are given preferred seating at his dining table, the best and most delectable selections of food (you notice none of the other thirty or so dinner guests are eating what you are) and his personal attention, you wonder what this is all about. Before you place the last bite of food in your mouth, you are told the unbelievable news- you will be the President of the U.S. This modern day scenario is exactly what happened to our Person of Interest, King Saul. 1 Samuel chapter 9 opens with the story of a man who had a good start but ended badly.

The prophet/priest/judge Samuel led God's people for many years but he was getting up there in age so it was time to think about a successor. His sons were not likely candidates because they were stealing the money from the temple, cheating the people out of the holy sacrifices that were meant for God and they were defiling themselves. So the people clamored for a king to "judge us like all nations" (1 Samuel 8:1-5). Samuel was displeased with their request and tried to talk them out of it but they would not heed the counsel of the prophet. When he took the matter to heart and inquired of the Lord, he was answered by God's reply to give them a king like they wanted but he was to warn them of the price they will pay for their fleshly choice of leadership instead of a divine one (8:10-22). Sometimes when we cry, beg, kick, and scream to have our way, God will let us. However, it will only be His permissive will at work in our lives, not His perfect one. God allowed Samuel to choose Saul and He allowed His Spirit to come upon him to anoint him and change him so that he could lead Israel as their king (9:17, 10:1-9).

Saul proved to be a king "permitted" by God but not chosen by God (1 Samuel 8:19-22). Outwardly, he was tall, strongly built and very handsome to the eyes. Inwardly, he was a man with low self-esteem and inferiority challenges. Upon hearing the news about his appointment to kingship, he did not see the possibility of such a position. He was from a small family that was not well known and not cut from the cloth of royalty (1 Samuel 9:21). How many times have we made excuses to God as to why we are not the person for the job? We come from the wrong side of the tracks, wrong color of skin, wrong bank accounts, wrong height, weight and the list can go on and on. On the day that Samuel announced to the people who their new king was, Saul was nowhere to be found but was hiding among the baggage. Some of the people did not even accept him as their newly appointed king (1 Samuel 10:20-27).

The people's choice of king also had trust issues, which caused him to make presumptuous decisions. He did not trust God and after a godly answer was delayed, he chose to take matters into his own hands, doing things his own way (1 Samuel 13:7-12). It is our lack of faith that drive the courses of actions that we take, making them seem right in our own eyes but they will lead to death and not life (Proverbs 14:12). Saul's hasty and unlawful act prompted God to seek his replacement, a man who would have faith and trust Him (1 Samuel 13:13-14). Without faith, it is impossible to please God. If we do not trust Him, we will not obey Him either.

The Amalekites were the longtime enemies of Israel. God gave instructions to King Saul for their ultimate and complete defeat. Instead of following those divine commands, Saul disobeyed. He selfishly kept the best spoils for himself and allowed the Amalek king to live. When Samuel questioned his disobedience, Saul made excuses and blamed it all on the people. His fear of people nullified his faith in God, which will always lead to disobeying Him. It is OBEDIENCE that God requires of His people and especially His leaders (1 Samuel 15:22). Fearing what people will say about you, think about you and how they see you is to seek their approval. You cannot fear man and God (godly fear is reverence) at the same time. People who are "approval addicts" cannot please God nor can they go where He leads for their fear of man will paralyze and limit them. The end result is …" Thus says the LORD: "Cursed is the man who trusts in man and makes flesh his strength, whose heart turns away from the LORD" (Jeremiah 17:5).

Saul's lack of FAITH, INSECURITY, FEAR of man, and lack of COURAGE ultimately cost him his kingship, his very life and the life of his son, Jonathan. His replacement was David, a man chosen by God, a man who had God's heart (1 Samuel 16:1). God's Spirit left Saul the moment it rested on David (1 Samuel 16:13-14) leaving Saul a man possessed with an evil spirit of suspicion and jealousy who made several attempts on his successor's life and estranged his own daughter and son in the aftermath. This KRACCKD POT's life left a collateral trail of damaged lives and people who were attached to him. Our lives are not our own and our choices are never just about us but can have dire consequences on those who watch, follow and are influenced by us.

You and I can have a grand beginning but it is how we finish that makes a difference. The choices and decisions that we make must be based on faith in God. Faith will bolster our courage and we will not be fearful or seek the approval of man. We will be secure in whom God has made us and called us to be. This is the journey of going from being a KRAACKD POT to a BRKNVESSEL!

TAKE ANOTHER DIP

In 2 Kings Chapter 5 we meet a man who is gallant, courageous, valiant and one of his king's favorite and most trusted soldiers. God's hand was upon Naaman and through him, gave Syria many victories in battles fought against their enemies. Nevertheless, there was one blemish to this mighty soldier's resume- he was a leper. Leprosy is a disease of the skin that causes sores to break out. It affects the nerves outside the brain and spinal cord. In addition, it may strike the eyes and the thin tissue lining the inside of the nose. The disease is known by the sores on the body and the deformities of the face, hands and feet that it causes as well. In Bible times, lepers were not allowed to be in the general population of people but were ostracized and set apart to live in leper colonies (Luke 11:17-19).

An Israelite servant girl of Naaman's wife told her that it was possible for her husband to be healed. He needed to see a prophet. When Naaman shared the hopeful news with his master, the Syrian king sent letters to the Israelite king requesting him to heal his faithful servant. But it wasn't the king that could do this and when he read the letter, he was distraught, tearing his clothes and accusing his Syrian counterpart of trying to "pick a quarrel" with him (2 Kings 5:7). Upon hearing the plight of the king, the prophet Elisha reprimanded him, "Why have you torn your clothes? Please let him come to me, and he shall know that there is a prophet in Israel" (v.8). He called and sent for Naaman to come to his home. However, it was not a personal word from the prophet himself that came to Naaman. A messenger of the prophet came out to the great man with instructions for his healing- a dipping in the Jordan River, seven times, and he would be healed. Instead of being grateful, Naaman became hateful and indignant. How dare the prophet give him a second hand message? Does he not know who I am? To add insult to injury, he wanted Naaman to wash in the dirty Jordan River. Were there not much cleaner rivers in his own country? (5:11-12). It is amazing that pride will not allow us to follow instructions even when those instructions will bring life and deliverance to our situations. We can think more highly of ourselves than we ought to and presume that people should treat us a certain way or we are entitled to places, positions and possessions. Therefore, Naaman went back home angry and still a leper.

Just when it seemed Naaman would be a KRAACKD POT, something turned his fate. His behavior and his response to the prophet was challenged, "My father, *if* the prophet had told you *to do* something great, would you not have done *it?* How much more then, when he says to you, 'Wash, and be clean'?" (5:13). Sometimes, that is just what is needed, a jolt of truth spoken in love. These were not strangers but people who loved, served and respected this great man. Moreover, this great man evidently loved and respected those who served him. He listened and he obeyed. He returned, dipped in the Jordan seven times, as he was instructed, and was healed, his flesh being restored, healthy and whole like a child's.

Here are a few points about "dipping". A servant girl was willing to take a risk and unselfishly suggested a solution for the man who owned her. She put his well-being ahead of her own. Naaman trusted her enough to heed and to pursue her counsel. It takes humility and openness to receive and follow through with the counsel of someone who may not be of the same socio-economics, culture or even age that we are. Even a child can speak wisdom into the hearing of their parents. No matter who we are in life and how great we may be there are "imperfections and hindrances" that we all have. There will be times when we have to face them and be willing to do something about them if need be. The answers to our dilemmas and trials may not look like or feel like the ones we want but we must be humble and VULNERABLE enough to trust and submit. God resists the proud but gives grace to the humble (James 4:6). This means He gives us what we need to surrender, yield and trust the "process" that often is the key to our deliverance.

Naaman shows us that HUMILITY and VULNERABILITY are the garments of a BRKNVESSEL!

I'M TOO OLD TO HAVE A BABY

A newspaper headline read, "60-year-old Austrian woman gives rare birth to twins." Still, another article entitled "10 OLDEST MOTHERS TO GIVE BIRTH" claimed that an Indian woman, wanting to give her husband an heir, had twins at the age of 70, making her the OLDEST woman in the world to have had a baby. Imagine swollen ankles, morning sickness, and probable weight gain on top of all the issues that an older body goes through. Not to mention, the labor of childbirth itself followed by diapers, baby bottles, and late night feedings at that age? Humorously, I wondered, when these women's children graduate from college, will they ask, "Whose child is that" when they hear the names of their children as they walk across the stage. Both women wanted children. Age was not an issue for them because creating and sustaining a legacy and seeing a dream come true was more important to them. However, they were NOT the OLDEST WOMEN in the world to have had a baby.

Sarai and her husband Abram were 65 and 75 years old when they first received the news that they would have children in Genesis chapter 12 and 13, "for all the land which you see I give to you and your descendants forever. And I will make your descendants as the dust of the earth; so that if a man could number the dust of the earth, then your descendants could also be numbered"(Genesis 13:15-16). The dilemma, however, was that the couple had infertility issues- both she and Abram were past childbearing years. So, after ten more years of barrenness and waiting, they came up with their own plan of how they would help God fulfill his. Surrogacy was prevalent in that day. When a woman could not conceive, another wife would take her place, become pregnant and that child would then be the first wife's. It was Sarai who initiated the plan," Now Sarai, Abram's wife, had borne him no children. She had an Egyptian maidservant whose name was Hagar. So Sarai said to Abram, "See now, the LORD has restrained me from bearing children. Please, go in to my maid; perhaps I shall obtain children by her." And Abram heeded the voice of Sarai" (Genesis 16:1-2). A son, Ishmael, was born to the Egyptian handmaid. It was the collateral damage of strife, jealousy and pride between the two women that caused Hagar to take her son and run away. Sarai blamed Abram for the "mess", causing a rift between them and heartbreak for him (16:3-6). How easy it is for us to come up with plan "B", "C" through "Z" when we feel like God is taking too long to do what He has promised. Then when our carnal plans do not quite turn out the way we want them, we look for someone else to point a blaming finger at. We create many Ishmaels because of impatience and a lack of faith. In addition, many relationships have suffered the blows of blame and shame because of premature and presumptuous decisions.

The sovereignty of God rules supreme. Ishmael was Abram's seed so God did bless him and commanded Hagar to return back home. No matter what we may do, God's will shall be done. Thirteen years later, He reaffirms his promise to Abram (whose name was also changed to Abraham and Sarai's to Sarah). Angels visited them to give the 99 and 90–year- old couple the news that they are going to be parents, "And He said, "I will certainly return to you according to the time of life, and behold, Sarah your wife shall have a son."(Sarah was listening in the tent door, which *was* behind him.) Now Abraham and Sarah were old, well advanced in age; and Sarah had passed the age of childbearing. Therefore, Sarah laughed within herself, saying, "After I have grown old, shall I have pleasure, my lord being old also?" And the LORD said to Abraham, "Why did Sarah laugh, saying, 'Shall I surely bear a child, since I am old?' Is anything too hard for the LORD? At the appointed time I will return to you, according to the time of life, and Sarah shall have a son." But Sarah denied *it,* saying, "I did not laugh," for she was afraid. And He said, "No, but you did laugh!" (Genesis 18:10-15). What do you say when you literally "laugh in God's face" because what He just told you sounds too good and too astounding to be true? Sarah's laughter is a reminder that there is hope even after all natural hope is gone. Unbelief, doubt and bitterness after twenty-five years of unfulfilled dreams did not taint her attitude.

Genesis chapter 21 opens with the fulfillment of their dream, Isaac, God's "child of the promise". Isaac means laughter. And it is laughter that God brings into a life that surrenders its frailties and limitations to trust Him to do the impossible. We are never too old to give birth. Never too old to nurse a vision and raise up a dream given to us by God. God will fulfill it and we will embrace it. Though it may tarry, we can patiently wait for God's timing because it is always perfect and on time. The Almighty God gave Sarah strength to conceive, "Through faith also Sara herself received strength to conceive seed, and was delivered of a child when she was past age, because she judged him faithful who had promised" (Hebrews 11:11). He will do the same for us.

Now that's FAITH…the way of life for a BRKNVESSEL.

EVERYTHING THAT GLITTERS AIN'T GOLD

Aaron, the older brother of Moses received a divine call at the same time that Moses received his. After the burning bush experience on the mount of God, Aaron in the wilderness met Moses on his way to Egypt. God assigned Aaron to be the spokesman for Moses to Pharaoh after Moses resisted with excuses, "Oh, my Lord, I am not eloquent, either in the past or since you have spoken to your servant, but I am slow of speech and of tongue....Oh, my Lord, please send someone else" (Exodus 4:10, 13). God responded in anger at the excuses and the refusal of Moses to trust Him. So He chose a replacement, Aaron, "So he shall be your spokesman to the people. And he himself shall be as a mouth for you, and you shall be to him as God" (Exodus 4:16). Whenever we feel that we are not capable of doing what God has asked and refuse to do so, we are susceptible of being replaced. God's will is going to be done, with or without us. So when Moses relayed the heavenly assignment to his brother, showed him the signs that God gave him and told him the message that they were to deliver, he agreed and accompanied Moses to confront the most powerful leader of the known world of that day. Before they confronted Pharaoh, they came before the children of Israel to let them know what God was about to do, "Then Moses and Aaron went and gathered together all the elders of the children of Israel. And Aaron spoke all the words, which the LORD had spoken to Moses. Then he did the signs in the sight of the people. So the people believed; and when they heard that the LORD had visited the children of Israel and that He had looked on their affliction, then they bowed their heads and worshipped" (Exodus 4:29-31). Aaron used his God-given authority to speak for God. With the rod in his hand, he demonstrated the power of God before the people and they believed. It is an awesome truth to know that whatever God asks us to do, when we are willing and obedient, He will work alongside of us as a partner. He gives us "exousia", delegated empowerment and authority to accomplish the task.

In the ten plagues that God sent upon Egypt, God secured the freedom of His enslaved children. Each plague refuted the gods that the Egyptians worshipped, (the Nile river god, the fly a symbol of the goddess Utachit, and Hek, the frog goddess of fertility) and powerfully taught the Egyptians that God alone was THE one and only true God. God used Aaron and his rod in the first five plagues to equip Moses. In the sixth plague of boils, the two brothers worked together. However, in the last plague, Moses worked alone. This plague broke the hardness of Pharaoh's heart and bought the freedom of God's people.

They were released and left Egypt after "spoiling them" (Exodus 12:36).

It was just a little over a month after the miraculous Red Sea crossing and fatal destruction of Israel's enemies that they forgot who God was. While Moses was 40 days in the presence of God, the people decided to choose another leader in his absence, Aaron. He insisted that they choose a god as well. At this request, they bought all of their gold jewelry to him and he made a golden calf image. He also built an altar and declared, "These are your gods, O Israel, who brought you up out of the land of Egypt!" (Exodus 32:4). A scene of idolatrous "partying" is what met Moses when he was told by God to hasten down from the mountain and back to the people. They had already broken the first three of the Ten Commandments that God personally wrote in tablets of stone Himself and gave to Moses. Those laws were thrown to the ground, broken into many pieces, grounded into a powder and mixed into water of which the people were commanded by Moses to drink. It was to Aaron that Moses turned to for an explanation of what had happened, "And Moses said to Aaron, "What did this people do to you that you have brought *so* great a sin upon them?" So Aaron said, "Do not let the anger of my lord become hot. You know the people that they are set on evil. For they said to me, 'Make us gods that shall go before us; as for this Moses, the man who brought us out of the land of Egypt, we do not know what has become of him.' And I said to them, 'Whoever has any gold, let them break it off.' So they gave it to me, and I cast it into the fire, and this calf came out." (Exodus 32: 21-24). How short our memories are of what God has done for us. How carnal we become when we are caught and then put the blame of our shortcomings on others (Genesis 3:12, 13).

Three thousand people lost their lives that day. Not because they deserved to but because a leader abused his God given power and authority. Aaron was left in charge. But his presumptuous and haughty attitude positioned him in a place where he over stepped his boundaries, falsely represented God, and led His people down a path of sin. When leaders fail and fall, followers pay the price (Exodus 32:25-35). God expects his leaders to lead in a way that glorifies Him. We must make sure that we continue in the same posture of humility that He found us in because that is one of the reasons why we were chosen to lead in the first place. Unfortunately, Aaron, never completely surrendered his will to the will of God. Instead, his way and his will superseded God's and in a moment of crisis and in the absence of the real leader, it all became known. He was set apart for God's service at the beginning but his choice to live and lead contrary to the purpose of God caused unnecessary "collateral damage". While his beginning showed great progress and potential, his ending was KRAACKD!

ANOTHER BAD HAIR DAY

A father's lack of validation for his son, a sister who lives her life as a victim raped by her brother, a brother who is killed by the rape victim's brother, a father whose son conspired against him orchestrating a coup to overthrow him as king, and a son who dies at the hand of a disobedient general in his father's army, is our focus today. It is the story of Absalom, the third son of King David by one of his many wives, Maacah (1 Chronicles 3:2). Absalom (whose name means "father of peace" but whose life was far from a peaceful one) was very handsome with beautiful long hair. He was strong, very charismatic and powerful. However, he was also a man of unbridled and uncontrolled passion whose fire burned hotly, consuming all who were in its path. David's second born son, Amnon (a brother from another mother), fell in love with and lusted after Tamar, his half-sister. Under the cunning advice of a cousin, he found a way to be with her but overcome by his lust, raped her. After he got what he wanted, he threw her away as used goods in spite of her plea not to do so (2 Samuel 13:1-17). Lust is a selfish desire that seeks its own benefits and fulfillment at the expense of others. Love on the other hand, benefits and fulfills others at the expense of the one who loves. When Absalom saw the torn virginal garments of his sister (she tore them herself as an act of shame and disgrace) and the face of shame she tried to hide with her hands, he consoled and took her in to the safety of his house, "And Absalom her brother said to her, "Has Amnon your brother been with you? But now hold your peace, my sister. He is your brother; do not take this thing to heart." So Tamar remained desolate in her brother Absalom's house" (13:19-20). David, the father of all three, heard about the rape of his daughter by her brother and was angry but kept silent. Absalom was silent too, but the end was just beginning.

For two years, bitterness and anger boiled in Absalom's heart. It gave him the fuel he needed to plot and carry out the revengeful murder of his brother, Amnon (13:23-29). Afterwards, he flees for his life and hides away in the country of Geshur for three years. David mourns for his son, not the murdered one, but the murderer himself. He was relieved that Tamar's brother, did what he felt was the right thing to do in avenging his sister's rape. David's refusal to step in as a father to rectify the situation, instead, turning a blinded eye to it, and then allowing Absalom to become the fugitive "fall guy", was the beginning of his son's downward spiral. The choices that we make or do not make with our children will affect them. We must not relinquish responsibility and accountability in being the stewards that God has assigned us to be over our children,

His heritage and godly seed. Before David's tear filled and regretful eyes, he began to witness the consequences of his own unbridled passion and lust many years before in the taking of another man's wife, impregnating her and murdering the husband to cover up the baby that was not his (2 Samuel 12:1-15).

David was convinced to bring Absalom back home to Jerusalem but he would not go to see him or allow him to come to the palace. He was still the estranged son, loved by his father but a guilty reminder of the father's failed parenting skills. Therefore, for two more years the son again felt the pain of neglect and rejection. This time he took it out on Joab, the general who was responsible for bringing him back home. Absalom had his fields set on fire when the general would not respond and intervene again on Absalom's behalf to his father, David (2 Samuel 14:28-33)

Second Samuel chapters 15-18 records the downward spiral of Absalom's conspiracy and overthrow of his father, the king. He grows a following and an army of loyal supporters who declares war on his father, King David, who went on the run for his life and the life of his friends and other family members. The rebellious and embittered son takes over the kingship at Judah. He makes a mockery of David and disrespects his leadership, sleeping with David's concubines on the roof of the palace, in full view of the people (this was the fulfillment of 2 Samuel 12:11). Counsel is given to him to pursue and go after his father. God's favor on David allowed him to have friends on the inside to help him win the war. Instructions were given by David not to harm his son but were ignored by the very general, Joab, who spoke up in Absalom's defense. Joab's hand personally defied the king. Catching his son in a precarious place, caught in tree branches by his hair while trying to flee on horseback for his life, dangling helplessly and defenselessly, Joab pierced his heart with three javelins, instructing his armor-bearers to finish the king's son off (2 Samuel 18:8-15). His body was thrown into a pit and covered with stones, unbefitting for the son of a king. David again went into a depressed and mournful state over his son Absalom. The people felt that the retribution that they put their lives on the line for in saving the king, recovering his throne and bringing justice to his treasonous enemies was all in vain. Joab rebuked David for his seemingly response of ingratitude, "Today you have disgraced all your servants who today have saved your life, the lives of your sons and daughters, the lives of your wives and the lives of your concubines, in that you love your enemies and hate your friends. For you have declared today that you regard neither princes nor servants; for today I perceive that if Absalom had lived and all of us had died today, then it would have pleased you well" (2 Samuel 19:5-6).

While it would seem that Absalom was one of those "good guys" gone bad because of his circumstances, he was a KRAACKD POT. He had no control of his unbridled emotions. Pride, arrogance, bitterness, unforgiveness, a lack of respect for authority and God, ate away at his heart and soul until all that was left was a heap of cold stones that covered his cold body. Yes, David, his father could be blamed just as much for the son's actions. But Absalom was still responsible for his own actions. We may not be able to control what people or situations do to us, but we can control our response. It is only as we keep our eyes on God, our hearts close to His and our hands in His, that we are able to be BRKNVESSELS.

JUST DO IT

Imagine attending a wedding with hundreds of guests. The bride and the groom have just finished being united in holy matrimony, sealing the covenant with a kiss and being presented as "husband and wife" to the applause of friends, family members and loved ones in attendance. The reception follows thereafter with beautifully colored décor and plenty of delicious food and drink. Everyone is enjoying the festive and happy moment, chattering away, congratulating the couple with well wishes and their prayers of success and happiness. Just as they are about to prepare for the toast, the servers inform the host that they are out of wine. Mary, who was one of the guests overhears and whispers in the ear of her son, Jesus, "They have no more wine" (John 2:1-3). The tone was not one of surprise, disappointment or sarcasm. It was a request. Only the mother of Jesus, who knew what He was capable of, would approach Him knowing that He could do something about the situation. Jesus' response, however was not one expected of a son to his mother, "Woman, why do you involve me? My hour has not yet come" (2:4). Why would Jesus be interested in the wine running out? What did that have anything to do with his mission and purpose in life? In fact, why would He care about a daughter's outright rebellion to her parents? Or the elderly couple's retirement fund which has been depleted and now they have to be cared for by their son and his wife? And why would it make a difference to Jesus if we ran out of time to make the last three mortgage payments on our business and now the bank wants to foreclose?

Mary looked at her son and turned away to find the servers. She spotted the host and the servers having a heated conversation and the host angrily walking away. She went over to the servers and said, "Do whatever he tells you" (2:5). When Jesus told the servants to fill the six 20-30 gallon water jars with water, they obeyed. And when He told them to pour some out and take to the host, they did so. When the host raised his goblet to taste its contents, he was surprised to find it filled with wine, wine that tasted better than what had been served to the guests earlier, "And he said to him, "Every man at the beginning sets out the good wine, and when the guests have well drunk, then the inferior. You have kept the good wine until now!" (2:10). Upon filling everyone's glass, a toast was made and no one knew they were drinking wine that not too long ago was only water.

That first miracle was not so much about providing wine for a wedding as it was about having Jesus being in the room. When He is present, nothing is impossible. There is no request too small or too big for His concern. If Mary had been offended by her son's response, she would have stopped where she was, shut down and refused to go any further with her request. The cemetery is filled with what "could have been " but because of a closed door, a resounding "NO" or an insurmountable wall blocking further movements, dreams and visions died with them. If the servers had leaned to their own reasoning and understanding, there would not have been the opportunity for them to see a miracle done before their very eyes and with their very hands, (yes, Jesus did the miracle but He used them to help bring it to pass).

"Brknness" is just humbly doing what you are told to do. When God speaks, we must move with the "cloud" and expect Him to "turn" some things around for us as well.

WHEN THE ROOSTER CROWS

In the darkness of night, money is exchanged from one hand to another. At a dinner table with friends partaking of a meal, they find out that one of them is a traitor. In the dawn of an early morning, a rooster crows as one man runs away crying and another with trembling hands places a noose around his neck. Our study continues in Matthew chapters 26 and 27.

For three years, Jesus did not just go about doing good and healing all who were oppressed by the devil. He also had twelve men that He handpicked, men that He ate with, slept with, laughed with, rebuked, encouraged, trained and gave assignments to. Each man came willingly alongside the Man from Galilee, leaving businesses, family, comfortable lifestyles, and the familiar behind. But even though Jesus knew intimately and personally each of His disciples, they did not really know Him. One such disciple, Judas Iscariot, was a thief (John 12:6). Yet Jesus assigned him to be over the finances of the group. Judas saw that the ministry was quite lucrative and the popularity of Jesus, for everywhere they went, throngs of people followed them seeking to be healed or fed. He greedily devised a plan to fill his own money purse and to make a name for himself. He knew that the religious leaders were jealous of, threatened by Jesus, and were trying to find a way to get rid of Him (Matthew 26:3-5). This would be his means to his end, "Then one of the twelve, called Judas Iscariot, went to the chief priests and said, "What are you willing to give me if I deliver Him to you?" And they counted out to him thirty pieces of silver. So from that time he sought opportunity to betray Him. (26:14-16). They say that everyone has a price that they can be bought for. When greed and lust for power are in the mix, that price does not have to be much.

Jesus' impending betrayal was no surprise to Him (John 6:70). It had been prophesied hundreds of years before, "I do not speak concerning all of you. I know whom I have chosen; but that the Scripture may be fulfilled, 'He who eats bread with Me has lifted up his heel against Me.' (John 13:18). It is a painful thing when the hand on the other end of the knife in your back is that of a friend or someone you love. Sometimes the people we reach out to help are the very ones who respond back with ridicule, abuse and betrayal. When Jesus announced that one among them was a traitor, the disciples all began to question themselves, wondering who it was. And when Judas left out the room, no one dared suspect him. After all, who could be more trustworthy than the treasurer could? (John 13:21-30)

In Matthew 26:57-67 we see the plot of Judas and the religious leaders unfold when Jesus is betrayed by Judas' "kiss of death" (what the Italian Mafioso calls it), arrested and taken away to trial. The disciples all run and hide for fear that they too would be taken. But Peter follows and stands outside in the courtyard of the Praetorium, the place of Jesus trial, before the Sanhedrin and Governor Pontius Pilate. He is spotted and recognized as one of the follower of Jesus by a woman, "Now Peter sat outside in the courtyard. And a servant girl came to him, saying, "You also were with Jesus of Galilee." But he denied it before them all, saying, "I do not know what you are saying" (26:69-70). And moving away from her, he was pointed out twice more, and at the crowing of the rooster, he looked into the face of Jesus and remembered His words to Him not long ago, "Before the rooster crows today, you will deny me three times" (Luke 22:60-61). Not far away from the courtyard, Judas Iscariot has second thoughts about what he had done and tried to return the "blood money" to his co-conspirators only to have it rejected. He throws the money down, leaves and hangs himself (Matthew 27:3-5).

Judas's actions were those of someone who was remorseful. Remorse is a feeling of the mind and heart when one realizes the brevity of something they have done or said. Remorse leaves you feeling guilty and condemned which leads to a dead end street (literally for Judas). But remorse is not godly sorrow. Regret and remorse may say, "I'm sorry" but it is only because I've been caught and exposed. It's a response from the head and not from the heart. Peter, on the other hand, when faced with his actions, responded differently, "And he went outside and wept bitterly "(Matthew 26:75). Godly sorrow is grief and sorrow of the heart. A heart that realizes it has hurt and pained the heart of God (Psalm 51:4). And the response is not of guilt or condemnation but conviction that leads to true repentance, "Godly sorrow brings repentance that leads to salvation and leaves no regret, but worldly sorrow brings death" (2 Corinthians 7:10). Repentance allows God to comfort and give grace. We know that Peter received grace because on the day of Pentecost, he led 3,000 souls to Christ!

A KRAACKD POT says, "I'm sorry" but a BRKNVESSEL says, "Lord, forgive me, a sinner. I repent for hurting you".

S.O.S.

"And when he heard that it was Jesus of Nazareth, he began to cry out and say, "Jesus, Son of David, have mercy on me!" (Mark 10:47)

Many of us are familiar with the term S.O.S., a distress code originally used by the navy and military when in a life threatening situation. It has stood for Send Out Succor (help), Save Our Ship, and Save Our Souls. Sending out a cry of distress is in order when help is needed. Today's Person of Interest is Bartimaeus, the blind son of a man named Timaeus.

Crowds of people always gathered around and along the paths of wherever Jesus walked and traveled. The miracles, signs and wonders done by Him preceded Him wherever He went. Moreover, His teaching was such that no man had ever heard before. One day as Jesus and his disciples were leaving the city of Jericho, a great crowd of people also began to follow them out of the city. The clamor and noise of the crowd, was heard by Bartimaeus, who sat by the roadside begging. We do not know much else about him but must assume that being blind was a handicap that perhaps prevented him from making a decent way of living. Either physical or spiritual issues that limited their quality of life handicapped many people of Jesus' day. When Bartimaeus asked what all the noise was about, someone told him it was Jesus coming by. Jesus, the miracle worker? Jesus the Son of God, Jesus? Jesus, the raiser of the dead? His mouth screamed out the name that rang in his head and heart, "Jesus, Son of David, have mercy on me!" (Mark 10:47). Some around him told him to be quiet. But he cried out all the more loudly, "Son of David, have mercy on me! (10:48). Suddenly, Jesus stopped dead in his tracks and said, "Call him". It is only when we come to a place of desperation and the end of ourselves, that we will call out to Jesus. There are some things that we must not and will not tolerate any longer. Things that have disturbed and interrupted our very lives. That's when we need to send a S.O.S., Save Our Souls!

Bartimaeus' S.O.S got Jesus' attention. The people told him, "Take heart. Get up; he is calling you" (10:49). And throwing off his beggarly outer garment (he knew he would not be needing it any longer), he jumped up and came to Jesus. That is what God wants us to do. When we are in His presence, He wants us to GET UP from the places of "blindness" and be willing to THROW off those hindering obstacles that have blinded us. Then we are to COME to Him. We are to come confidently and in faith, knowing that we will not leave the same way we came. Jesus directly asked him what he wanted Him to do for him. The man directly answered, "Rabboni, that I may receive my sight" (10:51). When we ask for prayer, we must be specific about what we want. God will give us the desires of our hearts as they line up with His will. It is His will that men be healed and delivered (Luke 5:12-13). The determination and faith of "blind" Bartimaeus caused him to take a risk and expect to be rewarded for it. No longer would his name identify who he was. A BRKNVESSEL was once blind, but DETERMINATION and FAITH caused the blinded eyes to be opened.

RIPPLE EFFECT

The names on the obituary were a total of twenty. And all of them had the same last names. What a tragedy, someone thought, that we are standing at the burial site of a whole family. Not only the persons themselves were buried, but their pets, their household items, and the houses they lived in were torn down and buried with them as well. We will look at the tragic story of a man who loved gold more than he loved God.

Israel was flourishing and victorious under the courageous leadership of Joshua, the successor of Moses. Joshua's loyalty and obedience to God (we will definitely study him later), gained a powerful victory at Jericho. God's general led the people around the city blowing their trumpets until the great walls fell. The command from the Lord was the city's total annihilation, "And they utterly destroyed all that *was* in the city, both man and woman, young and old, ox and sheep and donkey, with the edge of the sword" (Joshua 6:21). But before the infiltration of Jericho, Joshua had given a mandate about the spoils of that city," And you, by all means abstain from the accursed things, lest you become accursed when you take of the accursed things, and make the camp of Israel a curse, and trouble it. But all the silver and gold, and vessels of bronze and iron, are consecrated to the Lord; they shall come into the treasury of the Lord" (Joshua 6:18-19). What belongs to God belongs to God for His purposes and for His glory.

The next city of conquest after Jericho was Ai, a royal city of Canaan. The general sent out spies to survey the land in order to prepare a battle strategy, as he himself was given that mission some 40 years ago. Upon their return, they gave a report of victory, citing that it was small and sparsely populated, "Not all the army will have to go up against Ai. Send two or three thousand men to take it and do not weary the whole army, for only a few people live there" (Joshua 7:3). However, their presumptuous confidence led to the slaughter of thirty-six Israelite men and the army retreating in fear and despair. The unexpected defeat sent General Joshua to his knees and face before the Lord, wondering what had happened. As Joshua and the elders sought God for a reason behind their defeat, the Lord revealed, "sin was in the camp". Not only had Israel stolen what belonged to Him, they lied, and hid the "accursed things" among their own possessions. Therefore, Israel could not stand before her enemies, but turned their backs to run away in fear (7:10-12). Sin always causes us to run away from God and leaves us weak and defenseless (ask Adam & Eve). We cannot have victory over our sins unless we surrender in obedience to God. God's revelation to Joshua and the solution was one that the General probably did not expect. In the morning, every tribe was to be called out, from that tribe, God would choose a clan, and from that clan a family, and from that family, the guilty man. That man and all that belongs to him would be destroyed by fire (7:13-18).

Through God's process of elimination, Achan was chosen. Joshua admonished him to confess and tell what happened and he did so, "Indeed I have sinned against the Lord God of Israel, and this is what I have done: When I saw among the spoils a beautiful Babylonian garment, two hundred shekels of silver, and a wedge of gold weighing fifty shekels, I coveted them and took them. And there they are, hidden in the earth in the midst of my tent, with the silver under it" (7:20-21). When Joshua heard the confession, he sent men to the tent of Achan, finding the items just as he said, and brought them back, laying them out before the Lord. What happened next was God's prior sentencing of the guilty. Joshua and all Israel with him, took Achan the son of Zerah, the silver, the garment, the wedge of gold, his sons, his daughters, his oxen, his donkeys, his sheep, his tent, and all that he had, and they brought them to the Valley of Achor. And Joshua said, "Why have you troubled us? The Lord will trouble you this day." So all Israel stoned him with stones; and they burned them with fire after they had stoned them with stones. Then they raised over him a great heap of stones, still there to this day. So the Lord turned from the fierceness of His anger. Therefore the name of that place has been called the Valley of Achor to this day" (7:24-26).

Achan's story depicts the ripple effect of sin. God did not specifically point out Achan when he revealed to Joshua who the culprit was, He said, "Israel has sinned" (7:11). One person's sin can and usually does affect others.

It was one man's sin, Adam, that brought eternal death to all of humankind (Romans 5:12). Achan's love for gold more than for a Holy God cost the life of 36 men, destroyed the morale of the Israelite army and cost the lives of his innocent family members! His disobedience made God's word null and void and he disrespected God's leader. Compromise, greed and rebellion not only brought the death penalty to Achan, the guilty party, but all that belonged to him met the same fate as well. Although, it can be very difficult, sin and rebellion must be dealt with and removed from amidst a people or it will block the blessings and the favor of God.

    A KRAACKD POT'S actions will also KRAACK and affect the lives of those connected to him or her.

THE MAT

Jesus has been in town now for weeks. People have been coming for miles and miles to the places where He has shown up. Everywhere that He is, crowds gather early and there is never a seat or space to get near Him. Nevertheless, four men were determined that they would get to see Jesus. The life of their friend depended on it. Our Person of Interest is not one but four as we look at the gospel of Mark chapter two.

Capernaum was the home town of Jesus and the center of most of His preaching and teaching. The small town was on the north corner of the Sea of Galilee. In chapter one of Mark's account, Jesus preaches in this region, drawing His first fishermen disciples, Peter, Andrew, James and John who left all to follow Him. Jesus travels throughout that region, leaving a trail of healings and deliverances from demonic oppressions. Those who were touched by Him spread the good news about Him. So much so, that His arrival in towns was known before He arrived and people would travel near and far to see Him (Mark 1:45).

One day as Jesus arrived at a house He was invited to, many people standing outside the door of the house met him and once He entered inside, there was no room there either. As He began to preach, He had the eyes of those inside and the ears of those outside, seeing and listening to every word. However, the message was interrupted by falling debris over their heads and when Jesus looked up, He saw a man on a mat being lowered with ropes into the room. To His amazement, He looked up into the faces of four men who had torn a hole in the roof to lower their friend down through it, "Some men came, bringing to him a paralyzed man, carried by four of them. Since they could not get him to Jesus because of the crowd, they made an opening in the roof above Jesus by digging through it and then lowered the mat the man was lying on" (Mark 2:3-4 NIV). Jesus looked down into the eyes of the paralytic man and said, "Son, your sins are forgiven" (2:5). However, the religious teachers and others had thoughts in their hearts of blasphemy and criticized Jesus for His statement of forgiveness (2:6-7). There may be some people who will be excited and glad to see others healed or delivered. On the other hand, there will be those who only see the technicalities of how it was done. Tradition and legalism have strict rules that can inhibit and negate the power of God. Jesus knew their thoughts and addressed them, saying to the man, "I tell you, get up, take your mat and go home" (2:8-11). Taking up his bed, the man walked away as the onlookers praised God for this miracle that had never been seen before (2:12).

There are three things to note as we look at this account. The four men obviously had faith to believe that Jesus could heal their friend because they brought him to the house where Jesus was. When they could not get in, their faith gave them some options. First, they UNCOVERED (acknowledged) the roof of the house. We must acknowledge the anger, the bitterness, and the sins that stand in the way of our getting next to Jesus. Next, they BROKE THROUGH the roof. Breakthrough will only come as we acknowledge those areas that hold us captive and in bondage. Then the men LET DOWN the mat that the paralytic was on. The "mat" is whatever we have relied on and lived with for so long that we have become comfortable with it. It has become a way of life and a stronghold that is incapacitating our movement and our freedom to go forward in victory in Christ.

Jesus saw something. He saw the faith of those four men. He saw that they were willing to UNCOVER, BREAK THROUGH, and LET DOWN. As a result, their friend was healed and walked out in a completely different way than he came in. When we are truly delivered from a paralyzed state, we will walk differently. BRKNVESSELS find a way to break through every paralyzing obstacle in order to walk away FREE!

FOOD FOR FISH

Locked in a jailhouse is one thing. House arrest is another. But what do you do when your place of incarceration is in the belly of a huge fish. Instead of three meals and a bed, you get the stench of rotten digested fish food and a mattress of seaweed to sleep on for the stint of your stay. Our Person of Interest is found in the book that is named after him.

The Ninevites were a ruthless and sadistic nation of people who lived in the capital city of Assyria, Nineveh. For many years, these warlike people were the enemies of and fought with God's people Israel. The city was founded by Nimrod, the hunter who was instrumental in the building of the tower of Babel in direct opposition to God, leading a worldwide rebellion among the people of that day (Genesis 10:8-12,11:1-9). It was to this city that God commanded his prophet, Jonah, to go. It was this same city that God's grace and mercy wanted to save (Jonah 1:1-2). However, Jonah had other ideas, ideas of running in the opposite direction. Jonah knew that God, in his mercy and graciousness, would pardon the evil inhabitants of Nineveh. How could that be justice? How could that be the reward for a people who did not worship the one and only true God but idols that required things of them that were unholy and despicable? In Jonah's mind, Nineveh deserved destruction not salvation. It can be very easy to be the judge, juror and even the executioner of people who we may feel do not deserve God's loving-kindness. Our self-righteousness and self-serving motives will have us moving in opposite ways of God. Moreover, we will think that He is not "fair". In response, we run away from God and away from His call. Jonah ran to Tarshish (the opposite direction of Nineveh), boarded a ship thinking he was also leaving the presence of God (1:3). Having Jonah as a passenger on their ship caused a life-threatening situation for the crew. God sent a dangerous storm that began to tear the ship apart. The crew cried out to their various gods, threw cargo over the side into the sea but all to no avail. It was the captain who approached a sleeping Jonah, imploring him to call on his "god" for help as well. Still, as the sea tossed them back and forth, they decided to draw lots to see who the guilty person was among them, who was the cause of "god's" wrath, "Then the sailors said to each other, "Come, let us cast lots, that we may know for whose cause this trouble has come upon us" (1:7). Lots were cast and the lot fell on Jonah. The men demanded an explanation and when Jonah told them that he was a Jew and a worshipper of God, "who made the sea and the dry land" they were terrified, realizing they were harboring a fugitive from God. More often than not, our running away from God in disobedience is more than just about us. We can unwittingly jeopardize the lives of people who are close to us or those we have been called to serve. Jonah suggested that the men throw him overboard but they tried to row back to land instead of creating an even worse situation for themselves, the murder of one of the passengers. However, the sea got even rougher, as if calling them to do just that. Therefore, they did, after praying and asking for God's forgiveness, "So they picked up Jonah and threw him into the sea, and the sea ceased from its raging" (1:15). Realizing and acknowledging God to be God, they offered a sacrifice and made vows to Him (1: 13-16).

Once overboard and in the raging sea, God sent a huge fish to pick up Jonah. It was there inside the belly of his "living jail cell" that Jonah prayed, repented, and cried out to God for deliverance. At the Lord's command, the fish spit Jonah up and out. Where? Three days away from Nineveh, of course (Jonah 2). The command was given a second time, "Arise, go to Nineveh, that great city, and preach to it the message that I tell you. So Jonah arose and went to Nineveh, according to the word of the LORD" (3:1-3). Jonah's message of impending doom unless repentance took place, caused the king of Nineveh to proclaim a fast for both the people and the animals. His decree commanded that they call on the Lord and turn from their wicked ways in the hopes that God would show compassion and relent (3:6-10). And relent God did.

In the face of God's mercy and compassion, we find our Person of Interest, angrily leaving the city, and going to sit under a shelter that he made for himself to sulk, "But it displeased Jonah exceedingly, and he became angry. So he prayed to the LORD, and said, "Ah, LORD, was not this what I said when I was still in my country? Therefore,

I fled previously to Tarshish; for I know that You *are* a gracious and merciful God, slow to anger and abundant in lovingkindness, One who relents from doing harm. Therefore now, O LORD, please take my life from me, for *it is* better for me to die than to live!" (4:1-4). God provided a plant as shade for Jonah and then a worm to eat the plant. Under the scorching rays of the sun, Jonah went further down his path of anger and now self-pity, wanting to die. He expressed his anger over the plant (4:9). In the same manner, God expressed his disappointment over him, "You have had pity on the plant for which you have not labored, nor made it grow, which came up in a night and perished in a night. And should I not pity Nineveh, that great city, in which are more than one hundred and twenty thousand persons who cannot discern between their right hand and their left—and much livestock?" (4:10-11). God's mercy is without measure and His compassion never fails. He causes it to rain on the just and the unjust. He wants us to have compassion and mercy as well on those who do not necessarily deserve it. After all, we didn't either!

Our story ends with Jonah, a reluctant prophet and servant of God, who was KRAACKD with self-righteousness, anger, bitterness, the wrong attitude, disobedience and a wrong perspective of WHO God really is. God opened a door for him to be "brkn". In the belly of the fish, he was. But in the end, he chose to hold onto those things that placed him there in the first place. He chose not to TRUST and OBEY when God calls even when we do not understand or agree.

TO BE BORN OR NOT TO BE BORN

"It's a BOY!" the doctor announced to the joy of the mother and the father in the delivery room. The picture taking, texting, and phone calls began as the family announced the birth of the new addition to their family. There is nothing more exciting than the birth of a baby into a family that has been expecting and awaiting his or her arrival. In like manner, there is nothing more miraculous than being born into the family of God!

Nicodemus was a teacher of the Jews, a ruler and a Pharisee (one of the two ruling parties of the Jewish council (Sanhedrin). Unlike the Sadducees, who were wealthy aristocrats and far removed from the common person, the Pharisees were usually from the business and working class. They believed in the written and inspired word of God but they also held to their oral traditions that had been handed down since the time of Moses. It was these oral traditions that they strictly followed along with the teachings and instructions of Jewish TORAH (what Christians call the Old Testament), causing them to often be at odds with Jesus. It was the desire to know truth and to hear the words of Jesus, who many believed to be the Son of God, which caused Nicodemus to seek Him. However, in order not to offend or present a conflict of interest among his colleagues, he visited Him by the cloak of night, "There was a man of the Pharisees named Nicodemus, a ruler of the Jews. This man came to Jesus by night and said to Him, "Rabbi, we know that You are a teacher come from God; for no one can do these signs that You do unless God is with him" (John 3:1-2). Jesus, knowing the true heart cry of this religious leader, cut straight to the chase, crashing the limitations of his mind to reach his heart, responded, "Most assuredly, I say to you, unless one is born again, he cannot see the kingdom of God" (3:3).

To the mind of a natural and intellectual person, Jesus' response did not make sense. How can a forty-year-old man be "born again"? How can anyone return to the womb of their mother in order to be born a second time? The things of the spirit are unintelligible to a heart that has not been opened and a spirit that has not been made alive, "Most assuredly, I say to you, unless one is born of water and the Spirit, he cannot enter the kingdom of God. That which is born of the flesh is flesh, and that which is born of the Spirit is spirit. Do not marvel that I said to you, 'You must be born again' (3:5-7). No university degree, status of life, position in the political arena or community leadership can cause a person to be born again or to even comprehend what that means. Jesus fulfills the inquiring heart of this leader, who although a teacher of Israel, did not, could not understand that which is not taught in a book or even from the classrooms of a seminary, "Jesus answered and said to him, "Are you the teacher of Israel, and do not know these things? Most assuredly, I say to you, We speak what We know and testify what We have seen, and you do not receive Our witness. If I have told you earthly things and you do not believe, how will you believe if I tell you heavenly things" (3:10-12)?

In order for a person to understand, comprehend and receive spiritual things, he or she must be born of the spirit. It is an inward and miraculous change of our very nature and a new birth of our spirit that was dead before, that even though we were dead because of our sins; he gave us life when he raised Christ from the dead. It is only by God's grace that we are saved! (Ephesians 2:5).

Even though, our Person of Interest started out with uncertainty and a fear that shook his belief system, he came to the knowledge of and the acceptance of what was true, not to his head but to his spirit. He took a stand in the defense of Christ against his own council (John 7:45-52). And even later, he accompanied Joseph of Arimathea of the Sanhedrin Council (also a secret follower of Christ) when the two of them approached the governor, Pilate, who had sentenced Jesus to death, and asked for His body so that it could be prepared and properly buried in a sepulcher that was the personal one of Joseph (John 19:38-41).

Nicodemus is another example of a BRKNVESSEL, whose "brknness" of himself, his traditions, belief system, and even his relationships that could not be a part of "a new life" in Christ, made him whole, spirit, soul and body. Being "born again" is not based on anything we do or who we may or may not be. It is based on the hunger and thirst of a humble heart. A heart that realizes and acknowledges that I was born in sin (Psalm 51:5), lost, with a need for redemption. I need a new nature, a "new birth" into a new family, the family of God.

A BRKNVESSEL is born again!

THE BLAME GAME

Imagine living in the most beautiful place your heart could desire, the perfect environment, climate, food, and the perfect companion by your side to share it all with you. Our Person of Interest had it all. However, he threw it all away when he played the "blame game".

In Genesis chapter one, we have the account of the creation. In six days, God created, designed, arranged, made provisions for and prepared a perfect world. There was no place on earth more beautiful and picturesque than the Garden of Eden. We do not really know where the actual location of the Garden of Eden was, but we do know of the location of two of its rivers, Tigris and Euphrates (Genesis 2:10-14), which are in the Middle Eastern region of Iraq. These rivers helped to keep the garden watered and lush.

On the fifth day of creation, God created living creatures to inhabit land and seas. And finally on the sixth day, His crowning glory, man, was created in His image, "Let us make mankind in our image, in our likeness, so that they may rule over the fish in the sea and the birds in the sky, over the livestock and all the wild animals, and over all the creatures that move along the ground" (Genesis 1:26 NIV).

Adam was created from the dust of the ground and brought to life, both spiritually and naturally, by the breath of God (Genesis 2:7). He was given the responsibility of taking care of his beautiful home and its inhabitants, the animals, whom he also named (2:19-20). Dominion, authority and power were given to Adam over all that God had created. He had access to all that was within his reach, with one exception, "And the LORD God commanded the man, "You are free to eat from any tree in the garden; but you must not eat from the tree of the knowledge of good and evil, for when you eat from it you will certainly die" (2:15 NIV). While each animal had a mate, male and female, Adam did not. Therefore, God devised a plan to accommodate him. He caused him to fall asleep and while asleep, God took a rib from Adam, made "WOMAN" (man with a womb), and presented her to Adam as his wife (2:21-24).

In chapter three of Genesis, we learn of trouble in paradise-trouble from a misquoted instruction by the woman to the serpent. The misquote was her addition to the conversation that God had with Adam (Genesis 3:2). Unfortunately, the fatal blow came when the serpent convinced her that what she was told by Adam (who was told by God) was not true. With Adam standing next to her, they both ate fruit from the forbidden tree. Suddenly, their visual perception became self-centered instead of God-centered and they realized they were naked. In shame of their nakedness and guilt, they covered themselves. Later when they heard God walking in the garden, they ran and hid from Him (Genesis 3:6-7-8). In our feeble attempts to cover up our wrong, we often will run away from the presence of God. Sin exposes our nakedness, and the guilt, fear and shame makes us turn away from Him. To make matters worse, when God asked Adam what had he done and why, he blamed the woman," "The woman you put here with me—she gave me some fruit from the tree, and I ate it" (3:12 NIV). The beginning of the "blame game" continues with Eve, who blames the serpent.

Adam and Eve (her name after the Fall) lost their paradise home. This perfect couple became imperfect by sin, losing their spiritual lives, fellowship with God and ultimately, their natural lives (3:17-24). The sin effect has passed on to ALL of mankind as a result of THE sin of one man, "Therefore, just as sin entered the world through one man, and death through sin, and in this way death came to all people, because all sinned—" (Romans 5:12 NIV). The man Adam mismanaged God's creation, his wife, misrepresented God, all by failing to put God's Word first. He then refused to take responsibility for his own actions, shirking them and shifting the blame. Unfortunately, leaders who play the "blame game" cause many of the breakdowns and devastations in our homes, jobs, churches, neighborhoods and communities.

A KRAACKD POT will shift the blame for his or her irresponsible actions- actions that will always have and cause collateral damage to others.

CRYING BABIES AND CROCODILES

The shrieking cry of babies and the even louder wail of mothers is heard as their sons are snatched from their arms and thrown like garbage into the crocodile infested waters of the Nile River. As the front door is about to be crashed open by Egyptian soldiers on an assignment of massacre, the back door swings shut as mother, daughter and baby brother rush to the riverbank. Let us look at not one, not two, but three Persons of Interest.

Joseph was the prime minister of Egypt whose wisdom and godly plan preserved that nation from famine. He also preserved all seventy of his family members who he had brought to Egypt (Exodus 1:1). Years later by the time that Joseph and the generation of his brothers had passed, God had multiplied the Israelites beyond measure. Their numbers posed a threat to the current Pharaoh who did not know Joseph nor had any relationship with Joseph's family. His fear turned into chains of slavery for the children of Israel, who were forced into hard labor and bondage. Their hostile oppression caused God to multiply them even more. So did Pharaoh's paranoia and fear, "But the more they were oppressed, the more they multiplied and spread; so the Egyptians came to dread the Israelites and worked them ruthlessly. They made their lives bitter with harsh labor in brick and mortar and with all kinds of work in the fields; in all their harsh labor the Egyptians worked them ruthlessly"(Exodus 1:12-14 NIV).

Pharaoh's fatal blow was to issue an order, one that he thought would bring about an answer to to his dilemma of the growing Israelite population, "When you are helping the Hebrew women during childbirth on the delivery stool, if you see that the baby is a boy, kill him; but if it is a girl, let her live " (Exodus 1:16 NIV). However, due to the bravery and faith of two Hebrew midwives, many sons were saved, specifically one of them in particular.

A Hebrew couple, Amram and Jochebed, had a son. When the mother saw that there was something special about him, she hid him for three months. This was no ordinary child, she thought, as she looked into his eyes while nursing him. God had a plan for him. And she did as well. She made a small basket of papyrus; water proofed it with tar and pitch and wrapped her infant son in his favorite blanket. Placing him in the basket, she and her daughter, Miriam ran to the banks of the Nile River, the escape route for her son. Jochebed placed her son in the dangerous waters of the river and his sister watched from the side, following the little "ark" as it went God knows where. Only faith in a God Who is merciful and Masterful would allow a mother to place her child in harm's way. Only a young girl taught to believe in that same God, would follow the basket from a distance until it came to stop in the most unlikely of all places-the home of the child's enemy.

Timing is everything with God. So it was, at His appointed time, Pharaoh's daughter came to the river to bathe as she always did. However, today would be different. As she waded in the water, she spotted a basket in the reeds. Her servants went to retrieve it and brought it to her. Opening it, she saw inside a male Hebrew child, one of those on the "most wanted" hit list of her father, "She opened it and saw the baby. He was crying, and she felt sorry for him. "This is one of the Hebrew babies," she said (Exodus 2:6 NIV). Again, God's impeccable timing proved itself as Miriam stepped out of her place of watching and asked the princess if she needed a Hebrew nurse for the baby. The wisdom of God not only will bring us before the right people at the right time, but will also give us the right words to say at the right time as well. Miriam went to get Jochebed, who not only was given the charge to nurse the baby, but she received wages for doing so. She nursed him until the time of weaning and then she returned the child back to his adopted mother, who named him Moses (2:8-10)

Only an Omniscient and Omnipotent God could orchestrate a story in which a victim is adopted, raised, educated, and given full rights as an heir in the home of the victimizer. Only God could choose three brknvessels, Jochebed, Miriam and a Princess, who against the threat of death, against all odds, and even against the potential wrath of a vengeful and murderous father, would be used in His plan of saving one of the Greatest Deliverers of all time, Moses!

BRKNVESSELS will risk, sacrifice and trust God no matter the consequences. They trust and know that the Almighty is in control of it all!

START AT THE END

So you set out to lose 25 pounds. You set up a daily regiment of discipline, exercise, and a diet change. For six months, you stick with it. The hard work pays off when on the day you step back on the scale; you proudly see the number is 25 pounds less than six months ago. You accomplished your goal! You decide to celebrate by treating yourself to that new suit you bought and hung in your closet as an incentive to lose the weight. The payoff is even grander as you receive compliments about how attractive you look in your new outfit! Over the next few days you decide to skip a couple of workouts, the next week you eat a candy bar or three and for the next few weeks, you have been waking up in the late night hour for a midnight snack. One day that new suit you were able to wear after you lost the weight months earlier has gotten tighter...and tighter. Once back on the scale, you realize that the race you began well has now gone downhill and the ending is looking as if you never begun. Our Person of Interest started out in a blaze of glory until he read his clippings from yesteryear and decided, "I've paid my dues! I can slack off! In fact, I can change the rules of the game". Unbeknownst to him, he was no longer even in the game!

Amaziah was a king of Judah. This was the time when God's people were divided into the Northern Kingdom of Israel (ten tribes) and the Southern Kingdom of Judah (two tribes). While ALL the kings of Israel were wicked and idolatrous, Judah had a few kings who served the one and only true God. Amaziah was one of these who followed God but not wholeheartedly (2 Chronicles 25:2). He led great military exploits and won victories for His people. However, there was a time when after a capture of his enemies, he took their idols and set them up as his gods. God sent a prophet to confront the Judean king but he would not listen. Instead, he went to war with the king of Israel, who warned against it. His army was defeated and he was taken captive. He outlived his captor, King Jehoash, for fifteen years and then, finally, a group of assassins (2 Chronicles 25:25-28) killed him.

King Uzziah was sixteen years old when he succeeded to the throne of his father. His mother and father evidently raised him in the fear of the Lord, "He did what was right in the eyes of the Lord, just as his father Amaziah had done. He sought God during the days of Zechariah, who instructed him in the fear of God. As long as he sought the Lord, God gave him success" (2 Chronicles 26:4-5 NIV). It is the God given duty of godly parents to raise their children in and with the knowledge of the Lord. There is no greater legacy that can be passed down than that of our faith. Amaziah also passed along his military prowess to his son. Uzziah and his armies defeated the longtime enemies of Israel, the Philistines and the Arabs

(26:7-8). His popularity and his fame grew even as his building projects of fortified walls, towers, and water cisterns. He was a man who loved agriculture and God blessed him in that arena as well (26:9-10).

The resourceful king supplied his soldiers with all that they needed for battles. He also invented a device that allowed them to shoot arrows and large stones from the safety of tower walls to crush the enemy below. Nevertheless, as Uzziah's fame and power spread, so did the cancer of pride. It is easy to become prideful when God brings us much success if we are not careful. When we were small in our own eyes, struggling to make ends meet, our prayer life and walk with God was consistent, we were humble and our faith stronger. Success oftentimes has a way of pushing our chests out and puffing up our heads along with it.

The king took it upon himself to offer incense in the temple of the Lord. This was a duty reserved strictly for the priests. Eighty courageous priests, led by the chief priest, Azaraih, confronted the out of order king, "It is not right for you, Uzziah, to burn incense to the LORD. That is for the priests, the descendants of Aaron, who had been consecrated to burn incense. Leave the sanctuary, for you have been unfaithful; and you will not be honored by the LORD God." (26:18) Instead of repenting and turning away, the king railed on the priests in his anger before the altar of incense in the temple. Suddenly, when the priests looked at him, they saw that his forehead had broken out into leprosy, making him instantly unclean. God's word is clear about how we are to handle his called ones. David understood well, that though King Saul had lost favor with God, he was still God's anointed leader. He could not, would not put his hands on King Saul (1 Chronicles 16:22, 1 Samuel 24:5-7). The admonition is not just for our actions towards God's anointed. It also applies to the words we speak against them as well, a lesson that Miriam, sister of Moses, learned the hard way (Numbers 12).

Leprosy was the curse of King Uzziah until he died. He was king for 52 years. His reign began with military victories won by a highly trained and outfitted army, massive building projects, witty inventions, fame, and popularity. Sadly, it ended with this KRAACKD POT dying and being buried in a cemetery near (not with) his ancestors. In spite of what he did and what was written in the records of Israel, he was known for being a leper (2 Chronicles 26: 22-23). It is important how we start our race and how we finish. However, it is even more important what we do between the start (salvation) and the finish line (heaven).

JOB SECURITY

Two days after the funeral of Mr. and Mrs. Palmer, their three teenage children gathered at the attorney's office for the opening and reading of the will that the deceased couple left behind. Only two years before their tragic car crash, they sat in this very office preparing for a day that came much sooner than anyone would have imagined. In the unhappy and painful environment, with tears flowing and nose wiping, the contents of the will were read, revealing the desires of the parents to secure the future and comfortability of their children.

The Roman government ruled the greater part of the known world during Jesus' day. They were cruel and hard rulers, placing over the provinces, leaders who were often unjust and selfish individuals. In religious affairs, the Romans were polytheistic, worshipping many different gods and goddesses for everything imaginable. They had an aversion towards the Jews and their "one and only true God". It was the deplorable and tyrannical conditions of living in the Roman Empire that caused the Jews to look for deliverance and seek a leader to overthrow the ruling class. There were many unsuccessful attempts to overthrow them, so when Jesus came on the scene, with his teachings and bold and courageous confrontations towards the government and religious leaders, he was seen as the answer.

Jesus walked with twelve men that He handpicked Himself. They spent all of their waking and sleeping moments with Him, watching the miracles, experiencing the confrontations with the status quo and religious leaders, and seeing the crowds of hurting humanity come out in droves to follow this "man like no other man". They experienced firsthand the transformations that He made in the lives of people, bringing and giving them hope for the future. They marveled at his teaching "as one having authority, and not as the scribes" (Mark 1:22). In their destitute and downtrodden minds, they also saw Jesus as a deliverer from the oppression of their Roman oppressors. He would be the one to start a new rule, a new kingdom. With this thought of rulership, the disciples began to have heated discussions and debates about who would be the "greatest" among them (Matthew 18, Mark 9, and Luke 9). In Matthew 20, Jesus receives a visit from the mother of James and John. These two men, along with Peter, were often with Jesus when the other nine disciples were not. Peter was the one who walked on water and he was the one who declared that Jesus was Lord. James and John (along with Peter) were on the mount of transfiguration, seeing Jesus in His glory. The three of them were with Jesus before His arrest in the garden of Gethsemane. So it was natural for the men's mother to come to ask that her two sons be Jesus' "second in command" in his kingdom, "Permit these two sons of mine to sit, one at your right hand and one at your left, in your kingdom" (Matthew 20:21 NIV). Jesus' response to her was that there is a price to pay for what she was asking. There is always a cost for leadership. Many people want to be in control and exerting authority but do not realize the accountability and the responsibility that goes with it. Jesus answered, "You don't know what you are asking! Are you able to drink the cup I am about to drink?" They said to him, "We are able" (20:22-23). Little did they know that one of them would pay the price- with his head. The other would be exiled to the isle of Patmos, the place where convicts were sent by the Roman government, until his death.

The other disciples were angry with the two brothers when they heard this conversation. After all, they were a part of Jesus' group also. They deserved the privilege of having a seat of authority and leadership secured for them in the kingdom as well. But Jesus gave them an eye opener. While their focus was on an earthly kingdom, His was a heavenly one. The criterion for rulership in that kingdom was not who could rise to a high position of authority but who could bend to a low position of humility. The greatest in God's kingdom is the one who becomes a servant and a slave to all, "Not so with you. Instead whoever wants to be great among you must be your servant, and whoever wants to be first among you must be your slave— just as the Son of Man did not come to be served but to serve, and to give his life as a ransom for many" (20:26-28).

Some KRAACCKD POTS will try to toot their own horns and others will promote themselves by assigning self-made titles and positions, even going as far as to pay money to buy them. However, only God promotes, chooses and places us where He desires in His kingdom (Psalm 75:6). Humility is the key! Besides, our greatest security is in knowing that we have eternal life and Jesus has gone ahead of us to prepare a secure place for us so that we can be with Him forever and ever (John 14:3). That's SECURITY!

NOW YOU SEE THEM, NOW YOU DON'T

For a moment, you thought you were getting away. When the prayer of healing went forth, you received it and were healed. Then you went back to the doctor and his report said that the cancer has returned.

The children of Israel were the newly emancipated slaves from generations of Egyptian bondage. For 400 years, their backs were the targets of the lashes and whips of their oppressors. Jehovah heard their cries for help and deliverance and He answered them in the person of Moses. Moses and his brother Aaron, confronted the most powerful person in the known world, the Pharaoh of Egypt, and commanded him to set free God's people. The demand was met with much resistance at the cost of human and animal lives. God as an affront, sent ten plagues to the gods of Egypt. In their face, He showed them Who He was, the God of all gods. Nonetheless, the pharaoh's heart was hardened (as God told Moses it would be) and he refused to obey until the deathblow that struck his household, took the life of his firstborn son and the firstborn of every Egyptian family (Exodus 11). Only then did he "let God's people go" but not empty handed. For the rag tag millions of slaves "spoiled their masters" and went off into the desert with freedom and wealth (Exodus 12:36-36).

After they were gone, it was not long before the hardness of Pharaoh's heart returned. When he realized the source and labor of his country's wealth was gone, he changed his mind, "What have we done? We have let the Israelites go and have lost their services!" (Exodus 14:5 NIV). Six hundred chariots, horsemen and troops pursed the Israelites and came upon them as they were encamped by the Red Sea. In fear and terror, the Israelites cried out to the Lord. They soon blamed Moses and accused him of leading them on a death march. They began to regret the fact they had listened and followed his leadership, "What have you done to us by bringing us out of Egypt? Didn't we say to you in Egypt, 'Leave us alone; let us serve the Egyptians'? It would have been better for us to serve the Egyptians than to die in the desert!" (14:11-12). It can be an all too familiar response after we thought we were delivered and then IT comes back. We trusted God, did what He said to do and now this is the reward for my obedience, "I thought being saved meant I would be free from trials and tribulations but now I see I was better off before when I was in the world without Christ" are the thoughts of a defeated heart.

Moses spoke to the people to encourage them and to remind them that the same God who freed them will fight for them, "Do not be afraid. Stand firm and you will see the deliverance the LORD will bring you today. The

Egyptians you see today you will never see again. The LORD will fight for you; you need only to be still." (14:13-14). God then gave instructions on what to do. As Moses stretched out his hand over the sea, all that night the Lord drove the waters back with His mighty hand. The waters were divided with a wall on the left and a wall on the right and a path of dry ground in between. Hurriedly, two million plus people traveled between the walls of water on dry ground with the Egyptian army in hot pursuit behind them. Unfortunately, for them, during the last watch of the night (God often will answer during the last moments of our dilemmas), the Lord jammed the wheels of the chariots bringing confusion to the army, causing them to realize once again He was God alone. As they tried to turn and retreat the way they had come, Moses stretched out his hand again and the waters of the sea flowed back over the soldiers, their chariots and the horses. The entire Egyptian army was swept back into the sea as the Israelites watched in horror from the safety of the opposite shore. In the distance, they saw the bodies of the dead Egyptians floating in the water and being washed on the shore that they had just escaped from. It was then that the people reverenced God as God and trusted Moses, His servant and their leader!

God used Pharaoh to show His people what was in their hearts. They had a KRAACKD POT mentality because when their backs were up against the wall, they forgot Who made the wall and began to doubt and even wanted to return back to the places of their bondage. When we do not trust God, we will forget what He has ALREADY done for us and how far He has brought us.

We will blindly become accusatory of the leaders He places us under and "play the blame game" when things don't seem to work out as we planned. God's mighty hand will always prevail and He will always vindicate those He has called and chosen to lead His people.

GET YOUR HOUSE IN ORDER

In 2 Kings Chapter 18, we find King Hezekiah, one of the few kings of Judah who acknowledged and trusted God, "Hezekiah trusted in the Lord, the God of Israel. There was no one like him among all the kings of Judah, either before him or after him. He held fast to the Lord and did not stop following him; he kept the commands the Lord had given Moses" (2 Kings 18:5-6 NIV). His father, Ahaz, was a wicked king who led Judah in idolatrous worship. When his son, Hezekiah became king at the age of 25, he began the reformation of the people, destroying pagan altars, idols and the temples of the false gods (2 Chronicles 29:5). His bold acts brought about a time of revival for the nation.

In Hezekiah's fourteenth year of reigning, the king of Assyria threatened war. Upon hearing this, Hezekiah "tore his clothes and put on sackcloth and went into the temple of the Lord" (2 Kings 19:1). He also sent word to the prophet Isaiah, who assured him that Assyria would not prevail but be defeated by God Himself and its king would return to his homeland. True to God's word, 185,000 Assyrians soldiers lost their lives by the sword of the Angel of the Lord. King Sennacherib returned home and was murdered one day by his two sons as he worshipped in the temple of his god.

It was during this time that Hezekiah became terminally ill. The prophet Isaiah came to him with an order, "This is what the Lord says: Put your house in order, because you are going to die; you will not recover" (2 Kings 20:1 NIV). But instead of running away and hiding or refusing to accept the word, the humble king, laid on his bed, turned his face to the wall and prayed to the Lord he trusted in, "Remember, Lord, how I have walked before you faithfully and with wholehearted devotion and have done what is good in your eyes." And Hezekiah wept bitterly" (20:3). Before the prophet was out of the palace, God turned him around to go back to the king and to give him another word, "This is what the Lord, the God of your father David, says: I have heard your prayer and seen your tears; I will heal you. On the third day from now you will go up to the temple of the Lord. I will add fifteen years to your life. And I will deliver you and this city from the hand of the king of Assyria" (20:5-6). A medicinal application of figs was made, applied to the boils of the king and he was healed!

Hezekiah showed that a brknvessel will humble themselves, relinquish their own power and strength and pray to trust God for His (2 Chronicles 7:14). He did not lean to his own understanding but trusted God in all his ways (Proverbs 3:5). God rewarded his trust by answering his prayers, giving him successful endeavors and miraculous victories over his enemies.

A BRKNVESSEL will humbly keep their house under the inspections of the Lord. We must remain sensitive to the Holy Spirit when He reveals areas to us that need cleaning and realigning to the purposes and plans of God. Also, a posture of "brknness" (humility) will keep us trusting God for the possible when faced with the impossible situations of life.

THIS ISN'T BURGER KING!

For 40 years, Burger King's slogan was "HAVE IT YOUR WAY". Then in 2014, they changed it to "BE YOUR WAY". Over the years, some other slogans of the fast food chain have been, "Your Way Right Away", "When you have it your way, it just tastes better" and "Burger King, where you're the boss". Contrary to the thought of "having things you way", the first family of the Bible found out that in God's family, you "can't have it your way".

The cunning craftiness of Satan in his use of the serpent to deceive Adam and Eve, cost the first couple their God ordained home and purpose in life. The breaking of God's commandment, His one and only law, also cost the life of innocent animals. It was God Himself who substituted the animals' lives for the lives of Adam and Eve (Genesis 3:21, covering their nakedness (sin) with the hides of the substitutionary sacrifices). To make sure that the fallen and now imperfect couple did not eat from the Tree of Life and live forever in their perfect home, they were cast out of the Garden of Eden, which became guarded by an angelic being (Genesis 3:21-24). In time, some happiness returned to the couple when Eve gave birth to two sons, Cain and his brother, Abel.

Cain was a farmer working the ground and cultivating its produce while his brother was a shepherd. Our children may come from the same sets of parents but their walk and vocations in life may differ from one to another. Both sons would have been told about the sins of their parents and the great cost and price that was paid as a result. Adam would have taught the boys that God requires a "sin offering" as a necessity to maintain a right standing with Him. That is the only explanation for the fact that one day they both came to give God an offering, "In the course of time Cain brought some of the fruits of the soil as an offering to the LORD. And Abel also brought an offering—fat portions from some of the firstborn of his flock. The LORD looked with favor on Abel and his offering" (Genesis 4:3-4 NIV). But there was a problem. The Lord was pleased with and accepted Abel's offering but not Cain's. Why would God show "favoritism" towards one son over the other we may think? The answer is that God is NEVER a respecter of persons but He is a respecter of faith, "By faith Abel offered God a better sacrifice than Cain did" (Hebrews 11:4). Abel, by faith, obeyed God's instructions for how to approach Him and so did what was pleasing and acceptable in the sight of God. Cain, on the other hand, "brought some of the fruits of the soil as an offering to the LORD" (Genesis 4:3). There was no blood; there was no innocent animal to take the place of a guilty man. Neither brother knew then that God was paving the way and pointing His finger to another substitutionary Sacrifice that would take place 4,000 years later!

Cain's response to God's rejection of his offering was anger towards God and jealousy, hatred, and bitterness towards his brother. God called him to the carpet on his response when He said, "Why are you angry? Why is your face downcast? If you do what is right, will you not be accepted? But if you do not do what is right, sin is crouching at your door; it desires to have you, but you must rule over it" (4:6-7). God is clear and concise with his precepts, laws and ordinances. His ways are not our ways and His thoughts are not our thoughts. His rules are pure, true and righteous (Psalm 19:9). Contrary to God, our hearts are filled with unrighteousness and selfish motives (Jeremiah 17:9). We may think we can come to God in a way that seems right to us through man-made rules, traditions and ordinances, which is religion. But none of that will fly in the face of God when He has already given to us His way of approaching Him in relationship and fellowship.

Cain's bitterness and rage escalated into the premeditated murder of his brother Abel whose body he buried in the very fields he worked in. When God asked about his murdered brother's whereabouts, (God always gives us a chance to confess our sins first), Cain denied knowing and tried to justify himself, "I don't know," he replied. "Am I my brother's keeper?" (4:9). It will do us no good to try and cover our sins for they will always find us out and be revealed (Numbers 32:23). The cry of Abel's blood from the ground called for vengeance. God placed a curse on Cain that would cause him to be a homeless wanderer living a hard life on earth (4:10-11). The sentence was too great for Cain to bear and he begged for mercy knowing that his life would not be safe when people found out about what he had done. God in his mercy placed a mark on Cain that would protect him and a penalty of death on anyone who would try to kill him.

What may have started out as a simple offering to God ended with dire consequences when not done according to God's way. A KRAACKD POT will not acknowledge that there is a way that seems right in their eyes. Unfortunately, the end of that way is death (Proverbs 14:12). They will think that they are the "boss" and that their way is better. They will seek God and to please Him through the manipulations and fabrications of their minds and even with the "good works" of their hands. He is NOT Burger King! In order to please God we must come to Him in faith and in humble obedience!

POWER, PRESTIGE, POSITION

President Abraham Lincoln said, "Nearly all men can stand adversity, but if you want to test a man's character, give him power." A hundred years after historian Baron John Acton coined the phrase, "power tends to corrupt, and absolute power corrupts absolutely"; modern scientists claim that absolute power has similar effects on the brain as cocaine. Both raise the levels of dopamine, the brains' "feel good" system, which can be addictive, having both positive effects (confidence, energy, euphoria) and negative effects (arrogance and impatience) as well.

The Apostle Paul was converted to the "Way" (as Christianity was called in his day) on a mission to Damascus. This Pharisee of Pharisees, with papers in his hand authorized by the chief priests and the Sanhedrin, wholeheartedly did all that was in his power to oppose the name of Jesus and was responsible for imprisoning, torturing and killing those who professed to be the dead man's followers (Acts 26:9-11). But it was on his way to Damascus that the bounty hunter, saw the Light, and soon became the hunted himself (26:12-23). Years later, bogus charges and accusations were made against Paul by the high priest Ananias who turned him over to the governor Felix. In his custody, the Apostle Paul gave his testimony and pled his case of innocence several times before the governor and his officials. Felix, who knew about the "Way", did not see anything wrong that he had done. However, he kept Paul under guard with limited freedom for two years. His hope was to gain favor from the Jews and bribe money from Paul. Two years had passed and Festus succeeded Felix as governor (Acts 24).

Festus also saw no proof of the Jews accusations of Paul as he listened to the testimony of the Apostle. His desire was to please the Jews more than it was to do what was right, so he decided to send Paul back to Jerusalem to be tried by his own religious council. When Paul appealed to the emperor Caesar, Festus was afraid and held him prisoner. King Agrippa (the son of King Herod I that gave the order to have Jesus killed) and his sister Bernice came to visit the new governor, Festus. To gain credence for his actions, Festus told them about Paul and the dilemma he faced trying to prove his guilt. Therefore, the king wished to see and hear what he had to say, "The next day Agrippa and Bernice came with great pomp and entered the audience room with the high-ranking military officers and the prominent men of the city. At the command of Festus, Paul was brought in" (Acts 25:23 NIV).

Paul preaches to and gives his testimony before this powerful king and his entourage. The audience room was filled with high-ranking military personnel, aristocrats and prominent men of the city. This was all in fulfillment of the plan and purpose that God had placed on his life and prophesied about before his conversion (Acts 9:15). The passion, simplicity, and accuracy in which Paul gave his testimony, (proof of the risen Savior Jesus), caused Festus to accuse him of insanity, " At this point, Festus interrupted Paul's defense. "You are out of your mind, Paul!" he shouted. "Your great learning is driving you insane' (Acts 26:24 NIV). To this, Paul flatly denied his insanity but proclaimed his innocence and authenticity (26: 25-27). However, the heart of King Agrippa, teetered on the belief of the truth of what Paul spoke, "Then Agrippa said to Paul, "You almost persuade me to become a Christian" (v.28). Paul responded that not only was he hoping that the King would believe and receive but that all under the sound of his voice would be "persuaded" as well.

Almost is not good enough. However, almost is only as far as a KRAACKD POT will go. Power, prestige, and high positions in life will cause many to hold onto the earthly and temporary satisfaction that comes with these trappings. A KRAACKD POT will gain the world and will lose his soul in the pursuit of POWER, PRESTIGE, and POSITIONS.

"For what will it profit a man if he gains the whole world, and loses his own soul?" Mark 8:36

ONE LIFE TO LIVE

What would you do if you were told that you had a little less than a year to live? Would you rush to spend time with friends and loved ones? Would you try to make amends with people who have hurt or abused you in the past? Would you empty out your bank account and take that much needed but neglected dream vacation or buy that dream car whose picture is on the refrigerator door? Would you seek the face of the One who controls death and life-when and how it comes to your door? Our Person of Interest was given such news! To her horror, it would not be death by illness, sickness or disease but death my premeditated murder, a genocidal massacre of a nation of people.

King Ahasuerus had to look for a replacement for Queen Vashti. Three years into his reign in Shushan, he decided to celebrate the wealth of his kingdom by having a feast, which was attended by all his officials, nobles, servants and prestigious heads of the 127 provinces that he ruled. As he showed off his riches and kingdom splendor, he also included his wife, the queen, as an item of display. It was on the seventh day of the feast that the king had a little too much to drink, when he commanded her presence, wearing the royal crown (Esther 1:1-10). Now some Bible commentators have commented that the crown was ALL the king wanted the queen to wear, " to bring Queen Vashti before the king, wearing her crown, in order to show her beauty to the people and the officials, for she was beautiful to behold" (1:11). Whether this was the case or not, the queen refused to obey the command. Upon the advice of King Ahasuerus' trusted officials, she was dethroned as an example of what happens to women who do not obey their husbands, "for the queen's behavior will become known to all women, so that they will despise their husbands in their eyes, when they report, 'King Ahasuerus commanded Queen Vashti to be brought in before him, but she did not come" (1:17). When we are in leadership positions, our behaviors will always have an impact on those who are watching and who follow us, whether for good or for bad. But unbeknownst to all, the dethronement of the queen was part of God's purpose and plan.

A Jewish girl named Hadassah, whose name was changed to Esther to hide her nationality, was orphaned as a child and reared by her uncle, Mordecai, as his own daughter. Not only was she beautiful on the outside but on the inside as well. She was selected, along with hundreds of other young virgins as candidates to reign by the king's side. After a year of beauty treatments and preparations, each girl was permitted to take anything that she chose on the night she was to appear before the king. When it was her turn, Esther chose nothing but what the eunuch, who was her custodian, advised her to take. While we do not know what that one thing was, we do know that when one comes before the King of kings and Lord of lords, we can bring nothing but a pure heart and a broken spirit. Esther found favor with the king and was chosen as the new queen (2:12-17). God's choices are the results of His sovereignty. He does not ask counsel from anyone, not even the person that He chooses. It is by divine design and purpose that we find ourselves in the least likely of places and circumstances, chosen and orchestrated by the Almighty.

One month before the edict to annihilate the Jews and to confiscate their possessions, Esther was chosen as queen (2:16). Upon the counsel of her uncle, she was told to keep her identity a secret. Because her uncle kept tabs on her goings and comings as he daily sat at the gates of the palace, he overheard of a plot against the king. He relayed the information to his niece, who told her husband the king. The two conspirators were hanged and Mordecai was given credit by Esther for exposing the plot (Esther 2:19-23).

It was Mordecai who also heard of the planned massacre that was made into law at the suggestion of his enemy, Haman to the king ((3:12, 13). The wicked official of the king set out to take vengeance out on the Jews because of Mordecai's refusal to bow to him. The king agreed to the diabolical plan and word was sent to all the provinces decreeing it to be carried out. Mordecai sought out his niece once again to intervene on the behalf of her people, but this time the queen was hesitant about approaching the king, "Then Esther spoke to Hathach, and gave him a command for Mordecai: 'All the king's servants and the people of the king's provinces know that any man or woman who goes into the inner court to the king, who has not been called, he has but one law: put *all* to death, except the one to whom the king holds out the golden scepter, that he may live. Yet I myself have not been called to go in to the king these thirty days.' So they told Mordecai Esther's words" (Esther 4:10-12).

The main point of this story is that Mordecai reminds his niece that it was God who positioned her as queen for "such a time as this". Now was not the time to be silent because if she was, "relief and deliverance will arise for the Jews from another place, but you and your father's house will perish" (3: 13, 14). This heroic and courageous brknvessel, rose to the occasion, "Go, gather all the Jews who are present in Shushan and fast for me; neither eat nor drink for three days, night or day. My maids and I will fast likewise. And so I will go to the king, which *is* against the law; and if I perish, I perish!" (3:.16).

It was Esther's refusal to turn away from and ignore the situation at hand, even at the cost of her own life, which saved her people. She was willing to "give up" (sacrifice) in order to "go up". Only BRKNVESSELS will put the lives of others before their own instincts of self-preservation. Only they will see the hand of God move on their behalf to SAVE and DELIVER!

CRACKING UP

There is nothing like having your friends around you to encourage, strengthen and comfort you in the midst of a life crisis or tragedy. Their words can be like sweet music to your ears and a cool glass of water to a dry and parched throat. But what if instead of refreshing water, you had friends who gave you a drink of gasoline; adding fuel to a fire that was already raging and consuming your very existence? Our journey continues with three PERSONS OF INTEREST who were all "kraackd" up.

Job did not expect to have a day like the day when his livestock, his servants and finally all ten of his children were destroyed and killed. Each incident happened one right after the other with barely a moment for Job to recover from each horrifying blow. His heart was torn, along with his robe, after hearing the tragedies, but he worshipped God, keeping his integrity and refusing to charge God of being unjust with all that had happened. Finally, Job himself was attacked in his own body with a breakout of painful boils from head to foot. As he sat scraping himself with a broken piece of pottery, in the middle of a pile of ashes, his wife approached him asking,

"Are you still maintaining your integrity? Curse God and die!" (Job 2:9 NIV). Job, however, refused the folly of such a response towards God, "You are talking like a foolish woman. Shall we accept good from God, and not trouble?" In all this, Job did not sin in what he said (2:10).

Job's three friends, Eliphaz, Bildad, and Zophar heard about what had happened to their friend and set out to visit and comfort him. However, they were not prepared for the devastation, not even recognizing their friend when they saw him from a distance. As they got closer, they wept aloud, tore their clothes and sprinkled dust on their heads in remorse and anguish. For seven days, they were silent, feeling the pain and witnessing the horrific condition of Job. For seven days they offered a listening ear to their bewildered and despondent friend. Unfortunately, the silence was broken by accusations from them, of Job speaking about and seeing God incorrectly, behaving wickedly and thus deserving what had come upon him. At a time when Job needed words of encouragement and love, he got condemnation, misunderstanding, and criticism. It is very painful when we are misunderstood and falsely accused by people but especially so when it comes from those who are closest to us. Chapters 4 to 32 are filled with "gasoline filled" words of these three men. However, in chapter 32 and 33, a fourth friend, Elihu, a much younger and inexperienced man accusing them of self-righteousness and falsely representing God, contradicts them. Instead, he proclaims God's justice, majesty and goodness (chapters 34-37), opening a door for God to finally speak up for Himself in chapter 38. God will always have a remnant and the voice of one who sees Him from the right perspective and sets the record straight concerning Him.

God enters the scene in chapter 38, rebukes the men for questioning His justice, His Omniscience and His Omnipotence! Where were they when He created the earth, the heavens and all that they contain? Who gave Him counsel? Did the Creator seek instructions from the created? Who is the man that we would dare to question God or even try to tell Him how to do what only He can do? Does the clay tell the Potter what to do (Isaiah 45:9, Romans 9:20-21) and put Him on the stand by questioning and finger pointing? God confronted Job and finally, at the beginning of chapter 42, he responded to God in humility and repentance (as a Brknvessel). As for his three friends, "After the LORD had finished speaking to Job, he said to Eliphaz the Temanite: "I am angry with you and your two friends, for you have not spoken accurately about me, as my servant Job has. So take seven bulls and seven rams and go to my servant Job and offer a burnt offering for yourselves. My servant Job will pray for you, and I will accept his prayer on your behalf. I will not treat you as you deserve, for you have not spoken accurately about me, as my servant Job has." So Eliphaz the Temanite, Bildad the Shuhite, and Zophar the Naamathite did as the LORD commanded them, and the LORD accepted Job's prayer" (42:7-9). Job ended up praying for them and then God gave Job double restoration for his trouble.

It is so easy to judge and point fingers when the shoe is on the other foot. In a mode of self-righteousness, we can presume that because a person has suffered great tragedies or crisis in life, it is because they have done something wrong or are living in sin (and sometimes that may be the case, John 5:1-18). Nonetheless, God judges and knows. We are in no position to discredit Him or question why He does what He does, how He does it or to whom. Job's three friends were KRAACKD POTS. They started out with good intentions and the right heart, but they lost the true meaning of FAITH in God, UNCONDITIONAL LOVE, and HOPE!

HIDDEN FAITH

From 1941 to 1945, Adolf Hitler, created the Holocaust, one of the most deadly genocides in history. Hitler and his collaborators systematically killed about six million Jews, which included 1.5 million children and represented about two-thirds of the nine million Jews who had resided in Europe. Much of Europe was occupied and dominated by the Germans. In the Netherlands, as the persecutions of Jewish populations increased in July 1942, a young Jewish girl, Anne Frank, her family, and four other Jewish friends, went into hiding in concealed rooms behind a bookcase in a building where her father worked. And for two years they were hidden from their persecutors until they were found, arrested and shipped off to concentration camps from which only the father survived years later.

Joseph was a Jewish man who was engaged to a young girl named Mary. He was a good man and worked his carpentry business diligently. In Biblical times, a young man and woman would become "betrothed" through a consensual agreement mostly made through arrangements by their families. The bride-to-be would remain at home with her parents for several months while the husband would work to provide a home and means of living before they would actually come together as man and wife. It was during this time of betrothal when Mary gave Joseph the news (we can only assume that's how he found out) she was pregnant. One can only imagine the gamut of emotions that flooded the heart and mind of this man. Pregnant? By who? What will my family say? The neighbors, my friends? Not to mentions the deadly consequences that would be upon any woman who was found to be pregnant outside of marriage (Deuteronomy 22:13-21). Breaking laws can have serious consequences and the after effects can damage many lives centered around the offenders as well. But Joseph loved Mary and God's hand was in these "outside of the box" events, "After His mother Mary had been engaged to Joseph, it was discovered before they came together that she was pregnant by the Holy Spirit" (Matthew 1:18). Although revelation came to Joseph of the "how" this could be, there was still the question of the consequences for this violation of the law. So he decided to privately divorce Mary (he had the just cause to do so according to the law) which would only clear his reputation, still leaving her life in jeopardy, until God intervened, "But after he had considered these things, an angel of the Lord suddenly appeared to him in a dream, saying, "Joseph, son of David, don't be afraid to take Mary as your wife, because what has been conceived in her is by the Holy Spirit" (1: 20). God will intervene, especially when there must be a fulfillment of that which was promised before the foundations of the world.

Joseph took Mary as his wife and together they traveled to Galilee to a town called Bethlehem in order to be registered in a census and taxed according to a decree issued by Caesar Augustus. Mary was near her time of delivery. But because of the influx of people who came to be registered, there were no available lodgings for the couple. So the King of kings and Lord of lords had his humble beginnings in a place where animals fed and lodged (Luke 2:1-7). There will always be a way made for God to usher in His plans and purposes and He will provide the resources, often in the most unlikely ways. There were no fanfare, parade, or crowds of people at the birth of God's Son. Shepherds who were tending their flocks came to see that which had been told them by the angels. A couple of years later, a star led three wise men, bearing gifts fit for a king, to the house where the child was (Matthew 2:11).

After the wise men left the home of Joseph and Mary, they were warned in a dream not to go to Herod and disclose where the young child was. Instead, they were told to return to their home another way. When the wicked king realized he had been "duped" by the wise men, he ordered the genocide of all males, two years and younger, hoping that Jesus would be killed. The plan failed because God, once again, intervened, coming to Joseph in a dream, "Get up! Take the child and His mother, flee to Egypt, and stay there until I tell you. For Herod is about to search for the child to destroy Him." (Matthew 2:13). Once again, this man of faith obeyed God and saved the life of His Messiah.

Joseph raised Jesus as his own son. By faith, he surrendered his pride and his will to the perfect will of God. He knew that this Son was God's Son and this Son had a plan greater than the legacy of a carpenter (Matthew 1:21, Luke 2:41-50). God trusted and had entrusted him with the most precious Gift ever to be given. Sometimes, the very dreams that we believe in will have to be hidden; hidden from the dream killers and the faith stealers. However, when God's appointed time comes for the manifestation of that which we have believed, our faith will no longer be hidden. It will come forth as pure gold. That is the promise given to a BRKNVESSEL.

LET GO OF THE BANANA

In India, monkeys are in the category with other sacred animals. When the locals want to catch one, they anchor a bottle to the ground. The neck of the bottle is just large enough for a monkey's hand to fit in. Then, they put a small banana in the bottle, sit back and wait. Before long, a monkey comes by, sees the banana, reaches his hand into the bottle, and grabs it. Unfortunately, the monkey discovers that he cannot get his hand out of the bottle while holding onto the banana. There is loud chattering and squealing from the monkey as the person who set the trap walks up to him and places a burlap sack over him. In the darkness, the monkey releases the banana but it is too late. Our Person of Interest was rich, wealthy, from a prestigious background, popular and well known in the church. But there was one problem-he wouldn't let go of the banana!

Jesus had taken Peter, James, and John with Him to a mountain. It was there that they got to see the Lord in His glorified state and they also saw Elijah and Moses who spoke with Jesus. They wanted to make tabernacles in homage to the three men of God, but God's voice from heaven forbade this (Mark 9:1-8) declaring that it is Jesus, whom they should be listening to and following. When they arrived back to the house in Capernaum, he taught them about being humble and not to compete against one another, jockeying for positions of honor and prestige. He let them know that the greatest person in the kingdom of God will be the least one and a servant of all the rest (Mark 9:33-37). Positions of power and prestige are not important in the kingdom of God as they are only a means to an end. It is God who raises people up to lead, guide, and hold positions of influence and impact in order to make a difference in the world.

As Jesus was preparing to head out on a road trip, a man came running to him and asked him a question, ""Good Teacher, what shall I do that I may inherit eternal life?" (Mark 10:17). Hearing this description even of Himself, the Lord replied that the only One who was good was God Himself (v.18). He reminded the man about following the Ten Commandments. It was not that the commandments could make him (us) good. They were given to reveal the absolute righteousness and holiness of God and the impossibility of an unrighteous and unholy person to be able to obey each and every law (Romans 3:20). According to the law, if even one commandment was broken, guilty was still the verdict and punishment was still the price to be paid. We did not know that it was against God's law to commit adultery, to lie, steal or murder until the commandments were given and the "SPOTLIGHT" of God's word showed us that we were all sinners in need of salvation.

The young ruler insisted that he followed all of the law and has ever since he was a child. But Jesus looked at him through eyes of love and said, " "One thing you lack: Go your way, sell whatever you have and give to the poor, and you will have treasure in heaven; and come, take up the cross, and follow Me." (10:21). Sadly, that was not what the rich young man wanted to hear. How could he give away or even sell all of his worldly possessions? He had worked many years to acquire what he had, which also in his eyes, determined who he was. So he walked away from Jesus. The acquisition of eternal life was not as valuable or desirable as what he had in the bank, drove to work every day and went home to live in every evening. He would not let of go of the banana to live (make a living) instead of dying to make a life. God asks us what profit is there in gaining all that the world has to offer but lose our souls, our relationship and fellowship with Him (Mark 8:36).

Knowing God and having a life with Him NOW and FOREVER is what Jesus came to this earth to live and die for. We can have and should desire eternal life as something to be gained. Even if we have to let go of the banana (or the whole bunch) to have it. (Luke 17:33).

I HAVE A DREAM

"More than 5,000 symbol definitions that help you understand the meaning of your dream. Only YOU (emphasis added) can interpret your dreams, but this is the best way to start", read the introduction of a DREAM DICTIONARY. Many of us have dreams and many of us will often wonder, ask questions about or seek the meaning of those dreams. Our Person of Interest not only interpreted the dreams of others but had some of his own as well.

When the Babylonians rebelled against and overthrew the Assyrian Empire in 626 B.C. and the Egyptians armies in 609 B.C., they became the ruling world power of the Middle East. Jerusalem was conquered and the finest, most well educated and gifted youth were among the captives that were taken away to Babylon. Daniel was a young teenager when he and three other young men were placed in the courts of King Nebuchadnezzar to be trained, assimilated and prepared for use in his service. It was Daniel's commitment and faithfulness to His God and his Jewish upbringing that catapulted him (and his three friends) to a place of prominence in the Babylonian kingdom. Daniel had refused to eat the king's food (which was against Jewish dietary laws) and was able to convince the eunuch who was placed in charge over them to permit this intentional violation of the law. At the end of a set time given by Daniel, he and his friends were healthier and stronger than the young men who ate the king's food (Daniel 1:12-15). God will always honor our submission and our obedience to Him. He will not let us be ashamed when we choose to trust and follow Him.

After the three-year "processing" time, when the king examined them, "he found them ten times better than all the magicians and astrologers who were in his realm" (Daniel 1:19-20). The world's system may have silver and gold, fame and fortune, and those who are great at what they have or do. However, in God's kingdom, what is foolish, what is seemingly worthless or not up to par according to the world's standards, God will use to supersede what man thinks is "the greatest".

In Daniel 2, King Nebuchadnezzar has a dream that awakens him and does not allow him to fall back to sleep. He commands his magicians, astrologers and sorcerers to not only tell him the interpretation but to first tell him what he dreamt. Their response was a natural one, "O king, live forever! Tell your servants the dream, and we will give the interpretation."(Daniel 2:4). Nonetheless, the king was not moved. He gave them an ultimatum; tell the dream, its interpretation and be rewarded with gifts and prestige or risk the loss of their lives and the destruction of their homes (2: 5-6). The Chaldeans again countered the king about the impossibility of this, "There is not a man on earth who can tell the king's matter; therefore no king, lord, or ruler has ever asked such things of any magician, astrologer, or Chaldean. It is a difficult thing that the king requests, and there is no other who can tell it to the king except the gods, whose dwelling is not with flesh."(2:10-11). There was some truth in what they spoke for it is not the gods but GOD alone who can give a dream and its meaning. Unfortunately, sometimes the truth can make matters worse as it did for all the wise men of Babylon, of which Daniel and his companions were a part. The furious king enacted a death decree and his soldiers went forth and began carrying it out. When Daniel heard about the murderous decree, he questioned the king's captain about it and was told what had happened. He went to the king and asked for time so that he might tell him the interpretation. He immediately told his friends about it and they went to the dream giver Himself, "that they might seek mercies from the God of heaven concerning this secret so that Daniel and his companions might not perish with the rest of the wise *men* of Babylon" (2:18). God answered Daniel in a dream with the revelation of the king's dream. And when Daniel was brought forth before Nebuchadnezzar, who also asked about the dream itself, he let the king know that no astrologer, soothsayer or magician can declare it to the king, "But there is a God in heaven who reveals secrets, and He has made known to King Nebuchadnezzar what will be in the latter days". (2:28)

The young interpreter of dreams (soon to be a dreamer himself) revealed what was to become of Nebuchadnezzar and the world empires that would succeed him. His godly visions so moved the king that he fell on his face in obeisance to Daniel's God- acknowledging Him, "God *is* the God of gods, the Lord of kings, and a revealer of secrets since you could reveal this secret." (2:46-47).

God honored this young man because he was a BRKNVESSEL, completely surrendered and yielded to God. He was one of only a handful of Bible characters about whom God says nothing negative. He lived through the reign of three Gentile kings because of his CHARACTER, CONVICTIONS, COURAGE, and COMMITMENT to God.

WHO'S THE BOSS?

There is a saying that too many cooks in the kitchen will spoil the soup. There can be several cooks in the kitchen and they all can give input as to how the soup should be prepared but it is the head cook who must have the final say. Our Person of Interest not only did not understand that there is only one "boss" who is in charge but he also decided he would "make a soup of his own".

After the death of King Saul, his kingdom was divided into two loyalty camps. One held by his son, Ish-bosheth, who was installed as king over Israel by Saul's army commander Abner. David, who had served as king of Judah for seven years, headed the other camp. One day Abner and Joab, David's army commanders, and their men met at the pool of Gibeon to finally end the feudal war between the two kingdoms. Twelve men were chosen from each army to fight against one another. But when they all were killed, the war craze increased as the battle broke out among them all. King David's nephews (Joab, Abishai, and Asahel) were commanding officers in his army and were present for the battle. The Israelites were defeated and Abner ran for his life with Asahel in hot pursuit behind him. Abner called out to him to cease the chase and choose another man to pursue instead of him but Asahel refused to heed even after Abner warned him, "Stop chasing me! Why should I strike you down? How could I look your brother Joab in the face?" (2 Samuel 2:1-22 NIV). Abner had no pleasure in the thought of having to kill Joab's brother and risk the wrath of that man who already had a reputation of vengeance and taking matters into his own hand. In refusing to give up the pursuit, Asahel was met with the plunging sword of Abner into his stomach and he died on the spot. Joab and Abishai continued the pursuit until Abner's plea to cease stopped them. In the end, 360 soldiers in David's army lost their lives including Asahel.

There was a turn of events when Abner had a quarrel with Ish-bosheth over a woman. In anger, he rallied to the side of David. He secured the allegiance of the Benjamites and the elders of Israel to also make David king of Israel (he was only recognized as king in Judah) because that was the plan of God from the beginning, "By my servant David I will rescue my people Israel from the hand of the Philistines and from the hand of all their enemies." (2 Samuel 3:17 NIV). So they agreed. Abner traveled to Hebron to tell David the good news, who prepared a feast for him and the men traveling with him. They made a peace treaty and then Abner left to go and "assemble all Israel for my lord the king, so that they may make a covenant with you, and that you may rule over all that your heart desires" (3:21). As Abner exited, Joab and David's men were returning from a raid. When Joab was told that Abner had just left the presence of the king in peace, he confronted David, "What have you done? Look, Abner came to you. Why did you let him go? Now he is gone! You know Abner son of Ner; he came to deceive you and observe your movements and find out everything you are doing." (3:24-25). The commander left the presence of the king in a rage and with a plan to send after Abner to bring him to a meeting place. Unbeknownst to the king, Joab took Abner aside in private room as if to speak with him and there avenged his brother with a sword in the stomach of Abner (v.26).

The king later heard of the murder. He proclaimed his innocence in this sinister plot. He decreed a curse upon Joab and his whole family, "May his blood fall on the head of Joab and on his whole family! May Joab's family never be without someone who has a running sore or leprosy or who leans on a crutch or who falls by the sword or who lacks food." (3:28-29). The remorseful king also commanded all the people (including Joab) to fast and mourn for Abner. At his funeral, David sang a song of lamentation, weeping over the death of the innocent. His subjects, witnessing the grief of their king, followed suit. By his lamenting actions, they knew that their king was innocent of the murder of Abner.

David called Abner a "great man" (v.38). And that he was. Joab was not to get away for long. Solomon became king after his father David. The young king dealt with his three enemies, his own brother Adonijah, Abiathar the priest, and Joab. Joab knew that his time was up and attempted to run for safety into the temple to grab hold of the horns of the altar (an act of mercy). When he was ordered to come out, he refused and was killed there on the spot by Benaiah, a soldier who then took his place by the orders of King Solomon. (1 Kings 2:1-13)

Joab started out as a skillful, cunning and powerful commander. He was loyal to David and was a confidant and advisor to the king at one time (2 Samuel 19:1-7, 24:1-3). His lust for more power, pride, and an assumption that his relationship with the king placed him above the law, drove him to overstep his bounds. Selfish ambition, greed, and his vengeful heart, caused him to defy spiritual authority and to be presumptuous in taking matters into his own hands. He forgot who the Boss really was. God places leaders in authority and when we rebel against His appointments, we are KRAACKD POTS, rebelling against God Himself.

WHAT'S IN THAT LEADER?

Everyone knows that a good dish is one because of two things, the right ingredients and the hands that prepared the dish. Both of these are necessary to put a smile on the face of the eater and cause him to want more. We are going to look at someone who had just the right ingredients to produce the kind of leader that God wants all of His people to be.

The Apostle Paul spent a good deal of time as a prisoner for the Gospel's sake. From behind dark and cold walls and often chained between two prison guards, he penned the Epistles (letters) that make up two-thirds of the New Testament. When he was not in prison, he was traveling the known world, preaching, teaching, and raising up churches in the name of Jesus. On one of his missionary travels, the apostle went to the city of Derbe and then to Lystra where he met a young believer by the name of Timothy. Timothy was well thought of by his fellow believers and as Paul took note of this young man, he saw an emerging leader in the making. Timothy's mother,

Eunice and his grandmother, Lois, were Jewish Christians. His father, however, was a Greek who had not come to the faith of the rest of the family. Apostle Paul became acquainted with these two women, whose faith had been imparted and deposited into the young man, Timothy, "I am reminded of your sincere faith, which first lived in your grandmother Lois and in your mother Eunice and, I am persuaded, now lives in you also" (2 Timothy 1:5). When he left to continue in his missions, he asked Timothy to join his missionary team. As they went from city to city, the church grew in faith and in numbers (Acts 16:1-6).

Paul spent a lot of time investing in and mentoring Timothy. The young mentee traveled with the apostle on many missionary trips, preached in churches and was left to pastor an intimidating and difficult church in Ephesus after Paul was imprisoned. Timothy was ridiculed and criticized for his youthfulness and lack of experience (1 Timothy 4:12). Paul wrote two letters to the young pastor from prison, which are now referred to as the Pastoral Epistles. These letters contain instructions, counsel, and wisdom on how to lead God's people. In 1 Timothy chapter 3:2-13, we see the qualifications of a brknvessel leader. They must be BLAMELESS, quick to identify and repair any areas that may damage their integrity. A warm and HOSPITABLE spirit that welcomes all must be seen by and felt from such a leader. The ability to TEACH others and help them learn what it takes to become all that God requires is necessary in order to lead. Anything that will cause a leader to lose or blur their focus should not be an obstacle in the way, whether it is wine or any other intoxicating stumbling block that will be a hindrance preventing that leader from being sober, watchful and alert in every area of their life. A leader should have an approachable disposition of peace and healing, not violence and discord, to bring unity in the house of God and the relationships that He gives us. Another quality that a brknvessel leader should look out for is GREED. God will always provide what is sufficient and if more is needed, He will provide more. In order to manage the house of God, a leader has to be able to manage their own homes and families. And lastly, an inexperienced leader (and an experienced one as well) must be careful not to become PRIDEFUL when they are successful, thinking that it is by their might and by their power and not the Spirit of God that they are able to do what they do.

    In the Apostle Paul's eyes, Timothy was," a true son in the faith" (1 Timothy 1:2). His choice was based not on what was on the outside (external) but what was on the inside of the young preacher. In God's grace, He does not necessarily make His choices based on the talent, age, experience or skill of a person. However, He does base it on his/her FAITH, AVAILABILITY, HUMILITY, WILLINGNESS, and OBEDIENCE, the qualities of a BRKNVESSEL leader.

SPOILED FRUIT

Martin Luther King, Jr. was a prisoner in the Birmingham, Alabama jail when he wrote his famous, "Letter from a Birmingham Jail" in 1963. In this now famous letter, King confronted and addressed the moral leniency and the complacency shown by his fellow collegues in church leadership, who also often criticized his methods of obtaining equality and freedoms for all, especially people of color. MLK's call for justice from leaders was like another call from another "prophet" who God assigned to declare to His leaders that they must, "let justice run down like water, And righteousness like a mighty stream" (Amos 5:24).

Amos was a shepherd from a small town outside of Bethlehem. He also took care of sycamore fig trees. Figs were a food staple of that region and were eaten with many meals. His responsibility was to climb the trees to slit the figs with a knife so that the outer flesh of the fruit would ferment from the heat of the sun, making it edible. Even though he was called of God into the ministry of a prophet, he did not receive any formal education, never having attended the school of prophets in Bethel, "I *was* no prophet, Nor *was* I a son of a prophet, But I *was* a sheep breeder. And a tender of sycamore fruit. Then the LORD took me as I followed the flock, and the LORD said to me, 'Go, prophesy to My people Israel." (Amos 7:14-15). Prophesy is what this fiery preacher (often called the "angry preacher") did.

In Amos' day, the leaders were guilty of unfair moral practices towards the people. They were seekers of their own personal gain at the expense of the people that they were supposed to be leading. Leaders are to lead by an example of integrity and godliness, which attests to the character of their heart. Whenever they abuse the God-ordained power entrusted to them, they misrepresent God and misguide the people, causing them to turn away from Him. At first, when Amos dealt with the surrounding rebellious nations of Gaza, Damascus, Tyre, Edom, and Moab, Israel cheered him on but when he turned his fiery attention to "home", they rejected and ridiculed him for it. They refused to see the "beam" in their own eyes so that they could help to remove the "speck" in their neighbors (Matthew 7:3-5). While it is often easier to see the faults of others more clearly or even before our own, God calls his leaders (and his followers) to be objective. Every leader must make self-examinations under the watchful and revealing eye of the Spirit of God. Motives and reasons must be assessed to see if godly stewardship is the goal or selfish ambitions to build our own kingdoms at the expense of those who are less fortunate than we are.

God sent several punishments on Israel; withheld the rain, blasted their crops with blight and mildew, sent plagues and allowed their young men to die at the hands of their enemies in war, all to no avail, "Yet you have not returned to Me," Says the LORD. "Therefore thus will I do to you, O Israel; because I will do this to you, prepare to meet your God, O Israel!"(Amos 4:11-12). Just as God is a God of great mercy, He is also a God of great wrath against injustice.

In Amos chapter five, we see the injustices of the leaders, whose actions caused a ripple effect that spreads through the whole nation and especially those directly under their leadership. They refused to handle injustice by mishandling righteousness, sweeping what was right under the carpet. Whoever spoke up for what was right they hated and rebuked (v.7, 10). Unfair taxation of the poor lined the pockets of the leaders with proceeds that met their "greed" instead of the needs of the populous. Leaders who forget that they were chosen to help and not hurt and hinder people with their positions of power, will experience the wrath of God and will not enjoy the life they made taking food out of the mouths of others (v.11). Bribes were taken by leaders and the just were unfairly treated in and out of the judicial system (v. 12). Truly, we are living in the days where evil is rewarded and good is repulsed (Isaiah 5:20). God admonished the people to, "seek good, not evil, to hate evil, love good and establish justice at the gate in order to live" (v.14, 15).

Amos closes with a message of hope for restoration. But it will only come to pass after judgment. KRAACKD POTS will receive warnings from God that will expose and confront error and unjust behavior. If they are not heeded and received, true repentance will not be an option, nor will the mercy of God. However, if a change of heart, there will be a change of action and that's how a transition can begin towards being a BRKNVESSEL. The choice is always yours and mine.

DID GOD REALLY MEAN IT?

Think of your favorite book. A book that really had an impact on your life, causing some changes that you will never forget. Now think about what you would do if you had an opportunity to meet the author of that book. What would you say? What would you express? We have two Persons of Interest, who not only had a place in the first chapter of the greatest Book on earth; they met, walked and talked with the Author on a daily basis. There was one problem, however. They did not trust that the Author knew what He was writing about nor who they were in His grand scheme of things. We have talked about Adam and Eve when we looked at THE BLAME GAME. We saw how the consequences of our actions when they go against God's mandates and commands, will cause a chain reaction, resulting in collateral damage to those who we are close to in THIS ISN'T BURGER KING. A question for thought is, What causes us to not see ourselves the way that God sees us and how do we, how must we, respond when our true identities are under fire?

In Genesis 1:26-28, we read, "Let us make mankind in our image, in our likeness, so that they may rule over the fish in the sea and the birds in the sky, over the livestock and all the wild animals, and over all the creatures that move along the ground." So God created mankind in his own image, in the image of God he created them; male and female he created them. God blessed them and said to them, "Be fruitful and increase in number; fill the earth and subdue it. Rule over the fish in the sea and the birds in the sky and over every living creature that moves on the ground." Notice that God created man to be just like Him. He gave Him His nature, characteristics, spirituality, wisdom, and knowledge; all of Who He is. He then gave man authority, dominion and power over all that He has created (v.28). This was God's original plan and purpose for man. Not only did God orchestrate man's purpose but He also provided him with a home, food, companionship, and a relationship with Him, everything pertaining to life and godliness (2 Peter 1:3). God's heart was and still is, to have fellowship and relationship with us. How awesome that the Creator desires an intimate relationship with His creation. Once God created Eve from Adam's rib, He presented her to Adam as his wife, bone of his bone and flesh of his flesh, thus completing His creative purposes. Now fellowship would be possible on a daily basis as God visited the couple in the beautiful home He provided for them in Eden. God is our Provider. He makes sure that we are clothed more beautifully than the lilies of the fields and He supplies us with good things to eat. There is nothing that we need that He will not provide.

Adam and his wife were naked in the garden and unashamed of their nakedness (Genesis 2:25). Their lack of clothes illustrated that they were to be focused only on God, God-centered and not self-centered. There was no shame in being "naked" before God because they had a right relationship with Him and nothing came in between or inhibited it from flourishing. Nothing, that is, until they disobeyed. The Bible tells us that the serpent deceived the woman by telling her that God did not really mean what He said about the forbidden tree in the middle of the garden. Instead, he accused God of keeping something from His prized possessions and not wanting them to be like Him, "Then the serpent said to the woman, "You will not surely die. For God knows that in the day you eat of it your eyes will be opened and you will be like God, knowing good and evil." (Genesis 3:4). The irony behind the statement is that the man and the woman were ALREADY like God (god-like) after being made in His image. There was not anything more that they could be or needed to be. You and I were created just the way that God intended for us to be. God designed our weight, height, eye color, disposition, personality, etc. We are His workmanship, to be used for His glory and good works (Ephesians 2:10).

The one thing that God prohibited was the one thing that Eve desired, the tree in the middle of the garden that was able to open their eyes to know the difference between right and wrong. However, it was much more than that; it also presented the concept of choice. God wants us to choose between Him over whatever else may attempt to take His place. He wants us to choose His ways and not our ways, which seem right. The fruit that the forbidden tree bore was edible and would satisfy the flesh (lust of the flesh), it looked good to the eyes of Eve (lust of the eyes) and partaking of it would make her wise (pride of life). There were other trees in the garden as nourishing and as appealing to the eyes. Besides, she already had the wisdom of God. It is easy to want more than what we already have if we do not know that we already have it. Just the slightest bit of pride in our hearts will cause us to question WHO God is and if what He says He really means.

The last point is that immediately after Adam ate the fruit that his wife offered to him, both of their eyes were opened and instead of being God-centered, they became self-centered. Their nakedness that was a blessing became a stumbling block of shame and guilt. Therefore, they hid themselves. Hid from who? The One that created them naked and unashamed in the first place, "And they heard the sound of the LORD God walking in the garden in the cool of the day, and Adam and his wife hid themselves from the presence of the LORD God among the trees of the garden. Then the LORD God called to Adam and said to him, "Where *are* you?" So he said, "I heard Your voice in the garden, and I was afraid because I was naked; and I hid myself."(Genesis 3:8-10).

God responded by asking Adam "who told you that you were naked?" That was never an issue before. However, it becomes an issue when we disobey God in an effort to satisfy what feels good, looks good and makes us good but only in our own eyes or the eyes of the world. Our identity, which is found in Christ, is forfeited and misguided when we sin and lose fellowship and communion with God. We will no longer believe by faith that we are who He says we are, can do what He says we can do, or will be what He designed us to be. KRAACKD POTS are forever trying to please self and others. Instead of putting God first and having faith in Him, He takes second place right alongside doubt and unbelief. Instead of walking in authority and being as He is in this world, we will walk as victims and not able to be identified with Him. Did God really mean what He says? He did then and He does now!

FIVE THOUSAND PIECES AND MORE

Good cooks say that there is nothing more gratifying than feeding a crowd of hungry people. On the other hand, there is nothing more disappointing than cooking food for a crowd that is not hungry. One's search for food (or whatever it is that we may crave) is always predicated on how hungry we are. It is only then that we will look for a source to supply the need. Our persons of interest today are not one, two or three people but 5,000.

Jesus had traveled over most of the Judean country and many of its surrounding areas doing ministry. After the prayerful selection of his team of 12, he began to give them on the job training as they went about accompanying Him. These men were common folk who were beholding sights with their eyes and hearing sounds with their ears that never had been experienced by them or anyone before (Mark 2:12). All had left the familiar to follow a Stranger into the unfamiliar. They were compelled to follow this man, who spoke (John 7:46) and did things unlike any other. (Matthew 8:27). They were pulled by the Spirit of

God to follow Him with only a promise that, "I will make you fishers of men" (Matthew 4:19).

Everywhere that Jesus and His disciples went, there were crowds of hurting humanity following. Most of whom were the neglected, abused, tired, and weak citizens of society. They were broken and needed fixing, unloved, forgotten, needing love and a word that said, "I know who you are and have been where you have been". As Jesus performed miracle after miracle and they saw sign after sign, the crowds grew as people thronged Him, hungering after what He could do for them.

In Matthew 13, Jesus leaves his hometown of Nazareth because the people could not receive the miracles He did or the words He spoke. This was just Mary's "illegitimate" son, who grew up in our community, played with our kids and sat at our dinner table! They did not believe the claims about Him being the Son of God. Jesus arrived in Galilee only to hear the news about the beheading of John the Baptist upon the order of Herod, who was accused of adultery by the prophet (Matthew 14:1-12). He leaves to find a deserted and solitary place along the shores of the Sea of Galilee to be by Himself. The hungry crowds heard about him being in the area and went to where He was. Filled and moved with compassion for them, He healed their sick way into the late hours of the evening. Whenever there is a need, Jesus will see that the need is addressed and met. He expects His followers to do the same. Compassion will always bring about an action. It puts one in the place of those who are in need and asks the question, "What can I do about this?" His disciples asked that He close the healing service to send people into villages to buy food. Jesus said, "They do not need to go away. You give them something to eat" (14:16). But the only provisions available were five loaves of bread and two fish. Our perception and God's are as far as heaven (God's) is from the earth's (ours). While we only see what little we do have, God sees the much that it can become. Giving the disciples instructions, Jesus commands that the people be seated. Once seated, He takes the bread and the fish, looks up to heaven blesses them, breaks them and then gives them to the disciples to feed the hungry multitude. Not only were 5,000 men, their women and children fed but there were also twelve baskets of fragments leftover after everyone had eaten and satisfied. (14:18-21).

A hungry person will follow, search and seek after the resources to satisfy that hunger. Only God can satisfy the spiritual hunger in every man, woman, boy and girl's soul. All other resources will prove to be mere substitutes. Just as Jesus TOOK, BLESSED, BROKE and then GAVE the food, God's desire is that we yield ourselves to be TAKEN by Him, BLESSED by Him, and BROKEN by Him in order that we can then GIVE of ourselves to the hungry and hurting people of the world to be fed for and by His glory. Not only will we be satisfied but there will be more than enough left over afterward as well.

SNOW WHITE

In the old German Grimm's brother's fairy tale, the story of Snow White begins when a queen sits sewing at the window of the castle one wintry day. With her windows open, she pricks her finger and several drops of blood fall into the snow on the black window ledge. She looks down at the spilled red blood in the white snow on the black ledge and thinks how wonderful it would be to have a daughter as "white as snow", with red lips and beautiful shiny black hair. Soon afterward, she did have a daughter and named her Snow White. The queen died right after and her husband remarried. The second wife was very beautiful but wicked. She had a magic mirror that would tell her whenever she asked it, how beautiful she was and she was told that there was no one more so. That is until her stepdaughter, Snow White began to grow up. The tale continues with the queen's wicked plot to have Snow White murdered by a hired huntsman who instead defies her and spared her rival's life. The young woman then finds the home of seven dwarfs who gives her a safe haven and secure hiding place. When the evil queen discovered the deception, she sets out to take matters into her own hands. Twice her schemes to kill Snow White were thwarted by the dwarfs but the final blow came when she tricks Snow into eating a poisoned apple and the maiden dies. Jealousy and envy are dangerous partners that leave rottenness in the heart of an individual (Proverbs 14:30) making them capable of doing anything. Our Person of Interest started out with a pure heart (BRKNVESSEL) but her ending was not so much so.

When Pharaoh saw that the Hebrew slaves were multiplying and increasing, he began to fear for his life and the survival of his vast kingdom. In order to slow the growing population down, he devised a genocidal plan that would bring death to all male babies before they could draw their first breaths. Two Hebrew midwives were ordered to kill the male children after they were born. But the midwives' fear of God caused them to defy the Egyptian ruler, who sent his soldiers to take by force every Hebrew male child born and throw them into the Nile River. However, one child was spared. The mother knew there was something different about him and she prepared an ark of safety, placed her child in it, charging his sister to follow the little ark as it was placed into the Nile River going to "God knows where". God's chosen male child ended up in the arms of his enemies' daughter. And due to the faith, courage, and wisdom of his sister, Miriam, Moses was nursed and reared by his own mother before he was taken back to live as "a prince of Egypt". (Exodus 1-2). The plans and purposes of God will always take place when he finds those who are willing to go against the grain, to disobey ungodliness and in faith follow His leading even in the face of life-threatening consequences.

The spectacular story of God's promises and fulfillment to His people occur when, after 400 years of slavery, an eighty-three year-old Moses is appointed and chosen to confront Pharaoh with the true and living God and His command to "let His people go". Pharaoh's hardened heart would not do this until ten plagues, sent by God, wiped out Egypt's economic, social and agricultural systems and finally the life of every firstborn of Egyptian ancestry. God will always have the last say and the enemy will relinquish with much "collateral damage" left behind on his side.

The children of Israel exited Egypt but not without an infuriated Pharaoh and Egyptian army following in determined pursuit. Once again, they were no match for the mighty hand of God. The same Red Sea, which He opened for His people, causing them to escape the armies of Pharaoh on the dry ground of the seabed, backfired as a mode of destruction for Egypt. Horses, chariots and riders floated lifelessly in the waters before the very eyes of the newly freed Hebrews now on the other side of the Red Sea and looking back. Moses started out a song of victory and praise to God for triumphing over his enemy. Even before he could finish the song, his sister Miriam, the prophetess, picks up a timbrel and with the other women following, sang and danced victoriously before the Lord (Exodus 15:21).

Two years out of bondage, the children of Israel developed and continued with their pattern of complaining and murmuring against God and the hardships they encountered in the wilderness. In spite of God's provisions for their every need, their eyes looked and their mouths talked backward to the life they had in Egypt. Even as soon after God's miraculous move of supplying food in the middle of the wilderness (Numbers 11), trouble was stirring and brooding among the leaders, Moses, his brother Aaron and sister Miriam.

In the opening of Numbers chapter 12, we read, "Then Miriam and Aaron spoke against Moses because of the Ethiopian woman whom he had married; for he had married an Ethiopian woman" (12:1). These proud leaders went on to question why God spoke only to Moses and not to them. Were they not just as important and equal to him? The interesting thing is that their questioning had nothing to do with Moses' choice of a wife, but with God's choice of THE leader! Moses never defended himself because he did not have to. God heard the complaint and came down in a pillar of cloud, calling the three leaders front and center of the tabernacle. He called Aaron and Miriam to step out and forward. He chastised them with these words, "If there is a prophet among you, I, the Lord, make Myself known to him in a vision; I speak to him in a dream. Not so with My servant Moses; He is faithful in all My house. I speak with him face to face, Even plainly, and not in dark sayings; And he sees the form of the Lord. Why then were you not afraid to speak against My servant Moses?"(12:6-8). When you are chosen vessel of God, He will speak up for you and He will fight your battles. When the cloud lifted off the tabernacle, Miriam was leprous, white as snow (12:10). Aaron pleaded with Mose, the very person that they spoke against, who then pleaded to God for her deliverance. Shut out of the camp and away from the people for seven days, Miriam was then received back in and only then were the people able to move forward and continue on the journey.

A BRKNVESSEL became presumptuous and haughty in her thinking. Yes, this was Miriam, the older sister of Moses, who years earlier, trusted and had faith in the choice of God enough to help save her brother's life. And she was a prophetess of the Lord. Nevertheless, somehow and somewhere, her heart was tainted with pride, envy, arrogance, familiarity, and presumption. As leaders, we must be careful to always guard our hearts and keep them pure before God. Promotion comes from the Lord and if we are not careful, pride can get in the way (completely the opposite of why we may have been chosen in the first place). We must also be careful about how we speak and handle those whom God has CHOSEN (Moses), though we may be called (Miriam and Aaron). Our relationship with someone based on who we know them to be, can cause our eyes to be dim and our hearts to think we are their equal and have just as much right. Only God establishes and sets those lines of distinction and we should dare not cross them and become KRAACKD POTS. As leaders, not only will we pay a price but those that follow us will too!

CALLED OUT OF TIME

Growing up, we all have had dreams and aspirations of what we wanted to be when we reached adulthood. Schools were attended, grades were kept up, and colleges were entered and graduated from. Job interviews were set and contracts were offered for the career of a lifetime. Finally, a great life is the big payoff from years of blood, sweat and tears. Then suddenly a turn of events happens that blindsides us, leaving a pivotal tipping point decision to be made. Our Person of Interest was "minding his own business" when he looks up from his work and finds himself at the fork of two roads with the choice of leaving one and following the other.

A transition is always hard. The status quo, on the other hand, becomes a comfortable position, a mindset, and way of life. When the winds of change come about, they are often met with fear, uncertainty, and unchanging perspectives of resistance. In 1 Kings Chapter 19, God's prophet, Elijah found himself in a cave of pity after he defeated the evil Queen of Israel, Jezebel (1 Kings 18). It was in this dark place that God shed light and revealed His plan of victory and transition of power. Just when

Elijah thought, it was all over, God let him know it was only the beginning. He was given instructions about who to anoint as the king of Syria and the king of Israel (transition of leadership) and he was to also anoint the man who would take his place as well (19:16-18).

The son of a farmer was plowing the fields of his family, when he looked up and saw a man approaching, who threw his cloak on him and kept walking. He knew what this meant because he stopped plowing and ran after the prophet asking for permission to say goodbye to the familiar before proceeding into the unfamiliar. Elijah responded to the young man, Elisha, letting him know that was his problem and to do whatever he wanted to do (in essence "I'm following divine orders but it's up to you how you respond"). God's call may come from a person or a circumstance. We hear it but we must decide what to do with what we hear. Do we heed immediately? Or do we hesitate and procrastinate, feeling a need to tie up loose ends and say some goodbyes to the status quo. Elijah made his choice, "And he returned from following him and took the yoke of oxen and sacrificed them and boiled their flesh with the yokes of the oxen and gave it to the people, and they ate. Then he arose and went after Elijah and assisted him." (19:21). Elisha served Elijah for several years. During that time, he saw the hand of God on the older man's life and saw firsthand the power of God operating in the life of one who was totally surrendered to Him. Until one day, a change of events was to occur forever changing his life.

In 2 Kings Chapter two, we find Elijah moving about from place to place handling the business of the Lord. He is on his way to Bethel but this time instead of Elisha accompanying him as he always had, he asks him to stay behind. The younger man would have none of it," But Elisha said, "As the LORD lives, and as you yourself live, I will not leave you." So they went down to Bethel" (2:2). Twice more, Elijah tried to leave Elisha behind and twice more, Elisha refused. He knew that this day would be like no other day. Not only did he know, but also so did the other prophets who were in each of the three cities they traveled to, "Do you know that today the LORD will take away your master from over you?" And he answered, "Yes, I know it; keep quiet."(2:5). The two men stood on the banks of the Jordan as the older one took his cloak, rolled it up and struck the river and the water parted allowing them to go over to the other side on dry ground. It was the persistence of Elisha that caused Elijah, once they were on the other side of the Jordan, to ask what his last request was from him, "And Elisha said, "Please let there be a double portion of your spirit on me." (2:9). The request was a difficult one but not impossible. However, there would be only one requirement; Elisha had to SEE Elijah's departure. If so, the request would be granted (2:10).

As they continued on walking and talking, they were abruptly separated as a chariot and horses of fire from heaven caught Elijah up into a whirlwind. The only thing that was left behind was the cloak of the prophet that had fallen from him.

In no time, Elisha takes up the cloak that had fallen, goes back to the Jordan River to strike the water saying, "Where is the LORD, the God of Elijah?" (2:14). The waters parted and he crossed back over the Jordan in view of fifty eyewitnesses. This first miracle confirmed that the hand of the Lord had now transitioned from Elijah to Elisha as his successor. His second miracle was done in the Jordan Valley when he "healed" the bad spring waters of the city by using salt.

Scripture validates that Elisha did twice as many miracles as his predecessor. This BRKNVESSEL is a clear picture of SACRIFICE, OBEDIENCE, PERSISTENCE, DILIGENCE, and TRUST.

CARS, HOUSES, AND BARNS

A wife and her husband had been debating for three months now about adding on to the master bedroom suite. The wife complained that she was running out of closet space that was already jam-packed with an ever-growing collection of shoes, handbags, and designer clothes to match. Even though the husband agreed that she needed more space, he reminded her that their financial situation did not justify any house renovations. Instead, he suggested that maybe she had more than enough shoes and clothes. She countered with the argument that her job and status dictated that she look a certain way and she enjoyed how it made her feel also. Therefore, they were at a stalemate, not having been on speaking terms now for two weeks. Our Person of Interest had a similar problem. The existing storehouse was now too small for his ever-increasing "stuff".

In the life and times of Jesus, people were much as they are today. There were classes of people based on education, social status, and economics. Jesus encountered every class of person in His three years of ministry. His strongest confrontation came from those who were traditional and legalistic in their religious stand and those who were prominent in a society based on social and economic status. He told a parable about a man who had a very profitable farming business. Each year, his crops fared well and his pockets did too. Finally, one year he noted there was no more room in the barn that he used to store his incoming harvest and produce. Now, this may sound to you like a good problem to have, abundant blessings from a gracious God, who has blessed so much beyond measure that we run out of room to store His blessings. However, the man in Luke chapter 12, decided that he needed to tear down his old barns and build some better and bigger ones, "'What shall I do, for I have nowhere to store my crops?' And he said, 'I will do this: I will tear down my barns and build larger ones, and there I will store all my grain and my goods" (Luke 12:16). This is such a common response in a world where bigger and better seems to determine our prominence and importance. A bigger car, a bigger house, a bigger paycheck signals "I have made it" and I am successful. These material items are fine but when we wear and parade them as badges of success, it becomes a problem.

The first issue that our Person had to deal with was self-centeredness. Sadly, oftentimes, when people reach a certain plateau in life they get settled and turn inward. Hands that may have been outstretched to others and a heart that focused outwardly can turn inwardly, so why not "relax, eat, drink, be merry."(12:19). What once was enough can turn into an unquenchable hunger for "more".

The richness and prosperity that God blesses a person with are not to determine who they are in life for they are blessed to be a blessing.

A second issue with this KRAACKD POT is that pride grew out of a heart of self-sufficiency. This man decided that he had done well on his own and had more than enough to live off for a long time. Having a boastful conversation with himself about himself, "Soul, you have many goods laid up for many years", he felt that it was by his own might and power that he had accomplished what he had. In spite of our education, expertise, and knowledge, the truth of the matter is that God gives us the strength and power to become successful in life. You may say to yourself, "My power and the strength of my hands have produced this wealth for me. But remember the Lord your God, for it is he who gives you the ability to produce wealth, and so confirms his covenant, which he swore to your ancestors, as it is today" (Deuteronomy 8:17,18) in order that He may fulfill the promise to the spiritual children of Abraham, you and I (Genesis 12:1-3).

A final issue is a question of what should we really be storing up, acquiring and accumulating. Are we making investments in a heavenly bank account or an earthly one? The Bible has a clear answer for this, "Do not lay up for yourselves treasures on earth, where moth and rust destroy and where thieves break in and steal, but lay up for yourselves treasures in heaven, where neither moth nor rust destroys and where thieves do not break in and steal. For where your treasure is, there your heart will be also." (Matthew 6:19-21). It was obvious where the rich farmer's heart was. His focus and concern on being an earthly millionaire could very well leave him a heavenly pauper, "So is the one who lays up treasure for himself and is not rich toward God"(Luke 12:21). This KRAACKD POT'S wealth and success fell into the hands of someone else because very soon after the new barns were built, he died, leaving this world the same way he came into it, with nothing. (1 Timothy 6:6-10).

OIL FOR SALE

Debt is a very serious matter worldwide. Many businesses and individuals close and fold because they cannot pay their ever-mounting debt. In this nation alone, at one time, there were a little over 819,000 bankruptcy filings in a year. It is frustrating and can be a devastating feeling when your back is up against the wall as creditors, bill collectors, friends, and family members are demanding that you pay up the money that is owed them. The Person of Interest was truly up against a wall. Her husband had died and left her with unpaid debt. With nothing and no way to pay the mounting cost, her life and the lives of her children were being threatened. She was faced with a "pay up" or else.

Olive oil was a very important staple of the Jewish culture in biblical times. The oil of the olive was used for anointing purposes (olive oil was the main ingredient of the anointing oil). It was also used in the temple grain offerings. Kings and priests were anointed with it as a sign that they were specifically chosen by God for His use. And olive oil was used for cooking then as we use fats and butter today. The association of health, wealth and happiness was also attributed to one's possession of the oil.

In second Kings Chapter four, we have a dilemma that has come to the door of a widow. This woman was the wife of a prophet who had passed away leaving her with mountains and mountains of unpaid debt. Women in Bible times were solely dependent upon their husbands for their well-being and financial security. So when he died, so did the source of income and stability. This widow had no means to pay the debt off. There was a practice in those times to imprison those who were in serious debt until it was paid. Of course, they could not pay it while in prison so the burden and responsibility fell on the shoulders of family members. In worse case scenarios, such as the one this woman was facing, family members were sold off as slaves in order to ensure that the debt was paid in full, "And the creditor is coming to take my two sons to be his slaves." (4:1) Jesus was sold into sin to pay a debt not that He owed but that we owed. We had no possible means to pay the debt off. The burden of payment rested on Him, "having canceled the charge of our legal indebtedness, which stood against us and condemned us; he has taken it away, nailing it to the cross." (Colossians 2:14) and it was PAID IN FULL.

The widow shamelessly approached Elisha, the prophet of God, with her dilemma. She desperately needed some help (4:1). When help is the call of the hour, there is no room for pride or embarrassment. Oftentimes we will not ask for what we need or even acknowledge that there is one. We do not know exactly what she expected Elisha to do but the fact remains that she knew that if anyone could do something, he could and would. If it was money, she was expecting from him, it was not what she got. Instead, he asked her a very important question, "Tell me, what you have in the house?" Her response was "nothing but a jar of oil". It is amazing what "nothing" can become when we trust God with it. The prophet gives her the instructions to go and borrow as many empty vessels as she can from her neighbors, come back home, close the doors behind herself and her two sons, and start pouring the oil that she does have into the empty borrowed vessels. (4:3-4). As the vessels were being filled and set aside, she came to the last one and asked her son to give her another vessel. But he told her there were no more. Then the oil stopped multiplying because there were no more vessels to contain it. The widow went to the man of God who then gave her further instructions, "Go, sell the oil and pay your debt; and you *and* your sons live on the rest" (4:7).

Our story is a reminder to us that we all have "oil" that is valuable on the inside of us. Most of the time we are looking on the outside for answers that God has placed within. Each one of us has treasure in earthen vessels (2 Corinthians 4:7). It is only as we empty ourselves of "self", our ways, thoughts and selfish motives that we are filled with God's ways, His thoughts and eternal plans. BRKNVESSELS humbly acknowledge the needs in their lives and ask the God of heaven for His help in meeting every one of them. Then they selflessly submit and obey the plan that He has set before them. The giving out of our treasures will always prosper others who receive what God has given us to offer. There will always be more than enough for us to live off the overflow.

HOW ABOUT THOSE ANTS?

Some adults remember having a live ant farm when they were children. These live ants were housed in a plastic container filled with sand in which you could see their daily routine of gathering, storing food and digging tunnels for moving about. God's word praised the ants (wise) for their diligence and faithfulness to work. But it had just the opposite to say about the "sluggard".

A sluggard is defined as a habitually lazy or inactive person. Synonymous words are ne'er-do-well, layabout, do-nothing, idler, loafer, lounger, good-for-nothing, shirker, underachiever, informal slacker, slug, lazybones, bum, and couch potato. Either there are those of us who may know someone or we may ourselves fit the description above. Proverbs chapter 6 opens with warnings against foolishness, talking too much and laziness. In verse six, the lazy person is admonished to consider and compare their ways with the ways of the ant,

"Go to the ant, you sluggard; "consider its ways and be wise! It has no commander, no overseer or ruler, yet it stores its provisions in summer and gathers its food at harvest." There are some seasons of rest in God's kingdom but the season that we are in now is one of diligent and committed labor. Jesus said in John, chapter 9 verse 4 that, He must work the works of the Father who sent Him while He could because there was a dark time (his death and the persecutions that it would bring to His followers) that was approaching when no work could be done. We live in a dark world now (2 Timothy 3) and the child of God is called to go about to spread the light and good news of the gospel of Jesus Christ (Luke 4:18). No one has to tell the ant when to work. It takes the initiative to do so on its own (6:7). It works responsibly and prepares diligently for the present and for the future, cold, wintry season. There may be a tendency to want to slow down but the fields of the lost and unsaved loved ones, family members, co-workers, and neighbors are "white and ready to harvest" but the laborers (ants) are few (Luke 10:2).

The lazy person will not be awake or aware of the urgency of the hour. Instead, their eyes will be full of sleep. Their hands will be full of worldly and material possessions and desires; not open to working in God's fields to touch, heal and help the hopeless, "How long will you lie there, you sluggard? When will you get up from your sleep? A little sleep, a little slumber, a little folding of the hands to rest" (v.9, 10). The sluggard does not contribute to the world around them. No change, difference or transformation is brought to those within their scope of reach because they will make excuses for why they will not reach out (Proverbs 22:13). Just like salt, that has lost its saltiness, its flavor, and its ability to preserve decay is no longer any good and only fit to be thrown out, the sluggard's end will be that of poverty, lack, and uselessness. This is foolishness and the behavior of a KRRACKD POT.

NETS AND FISHES

Fishing requires time, some skill and a lot of patience. In Biblical times, it was one of the main professions of that culture. In Luke chapter five, Jesus was teaching on the shores of Lake Gennesaret to a large crowd of people. He noticed two boats left at the water's edge by their owners and got an idea. He got into one of the boats that belonged to Simon and asked him to push out from the shore. It was from this new vantage point that He taught the people. Jesus also had another lesson to teach.

When he finished speaking, he said to Simon, "put out into the deep water, and let down the nets for a catch" (Luke 5:4 NIV). After a long and unproductive day, Simon let him know that there was not anything caught. Nevertheless, a glimmer of hope shone in his heart as he then replied, "but because you say so, I will let down the nets". Sometimes we will exert great physical effort and prowess to accomplish a task only to have it fail or blow up in our face. The natural response is to give up or walk away. Instead, that is the time to take a moment and consider the request of the Lord when He speaks to us to try again. Simon's obedience paid off. This time the catch was so great that the nets began to break. The men needed the help of their partners with the haul and even then, the boats began to sink from being filled up with fish. (4:6-7) Overwhelmed and frightened, Simon fell at Jesus' feet, "go away from me, Lord I am a sinful man", he replied. The Lord reassuring him, let him know from this point on, he would be catching men (4:8-10).

There is another account in John chapter 21. This time it occurs after the death, burial, and resurrection of Jesus. Disillusioned and disappointed at the outcome of what seemed to be three years of a wasteful time, (the disciples spent three years with Jesus expecting a new kingdom and leadership), at Simon's leading, they decide to go fishing. However, after working all night their boats were still empty. Early in the morning, they get a surprise question from someone that at first, they did not recognize, "friends, haven't you any fish?" (John 21:4-5). When "no" was their answer, they were given instructions, "throw your net on the right side of the boat and you will find some". And find some they did. They were unable to haul the net into their boat. That is when they recognized the "stranger". It was the Lord! This time instead of Peter turning away from the Lord, he jumped in the water and swam to shore where He was. A fire was already burning ready for the morning breakfast of fish. Unlike the time before, this time, the nets did not tear with the great haul of fish. Even though we may be used to doing the same thing one way, God's specific instructions and His TIMING alone can make the old way, a new and improved one if we are willing to "let down our nets" again!

What changed Simon and made him a BRKNVESSEL? He had been with Jesus for three years witnessing His power, might, and authority. He had a revelation that this was no ordinary man (Matthew 16:16). His perception of who Jesus was and his mindset shifted. So much so, that he had a greater capacity to hold onto and to keep what the Lord had given him.

Having a revelation as given by the Holy Spirit of God, changes our perspective of Him and all that pertains to His kingdom. Kingdom truths will bring us to a place of greater capacity (faith) and we will be able to receive the greater promises. Only BRKNVESSELS can fish for men!

A MAN AND HIS BOAT

One of the most disheartening verses in Scripture is found in Genesis chapter six, "And the LORD regretted that he had made man on the earth, and it grieved him to his heart. So the LORD said, "I will blot out man whom I have created from the face of the land, man and animals and creeping things and birds of the heavens, for I am sorry that I have made them." (Genesis 6-7). The earth and the people in it were no longer God's pride and joy but our Person of Interest was chosen to make a difference in his wicked world and to change it from the inside of a boat.

Ever since the Fall of Adam and Eve that birthed sin in the world, man was determined to live according to his ways and principles, which always will be contrary to God's. This was the collateral damage of one man's sin that infected the whole human race. Adam's nature was in the DNA of everyone who was born then and now (Romans 5:12). The generations that followed his banishment from the home that God had prepared for him and his wife, Eve, only had intentions of evil and the evil corrupted humankind and the animal kingdom as well. God's decision to destroy man came because of His justice and judgments against sin. However, His mercy and grace appeared in His choice of the man Noah, who "walked with God and found favor in his eyes" (6:8-9). He was not a perfect man but he feared God, believed God, trusted and obeyed God. In a generation of lawlessness and wickedness, this one man stood out against the tide of unrighteousness to swim upstream in the river of righteousness. This is what draws and pleases the heart of God (Hebrews 11:6). He is forever looking for a man or a woman, who will dare not be conformed to the world's standards. Even though in the world, he or she will not live like the world. Instead, they will obey and walk with Him in this world to make a difference in it for His glory.

Noah was given the decree of God's judgment and His instructions that would not only save him but his wife, three sons, their wives and animal life. The means of God's salvation was an ark, a huge wooden "ship" that would be filled with the lives that God chose to save. Noah was about 500 years when he first got his orders and the ark was completed 100 years later as God commanded it to be. Can you imagine the words and the reactions of the people as Noah "preached" about the coming judgment by a flood? No one believed or took him seriously as is the general response to modern day prophets and evangelists who proclaim warnings of a coming king and judge but also giving a message of hope and salvation for those who will hear and heed. Unfortunately, when the first raindrops began to fall, the only human inhabitants in the ark were Noah and his family. Noah obeyed God, gathering the specified numbers and genders of animals into the ark with them as well. God himself shut the door of the ark. And for forty days and nights, the fountains of the deep burst and the heavens were opened. Flood levels prevailed above the heights of mountains and all flesh that breathed air died. (7:11-21). One year later, on the twenty-seventh day of the first month, Noah, his family and the animals exited the ark. Noah built an altar to offer a sacrifice to God and God entered a covenant with him. (Genesis 8-9).

The wages of sin, which is death, requires a just sacrifice (Romans 6:23). When God made a covenant with Noah, He gave up His right to destroy the earth by water. His sign is the rainbow, a continual reminder of His covenant and His word to humankind and the animal kingdom. Noah also sacrificed. He had to give up everything that he had ever known, his old life, friends, and the world that he lived in order to start over again. Sacrifice is the road to success in God's kingdom. Noah's ark was just a "shadow" of Jesus, THE "ARK" Himself. He would not only just save a family but the families of the world (in fulfillment of God's covenant to Abraham in Genesis 22:18). In a world that is selfish, self-centered, anti-Christ and dying, God is calling BRKNVESSELS to RISE up, and GIVE up, in order to GO up. He is sending out a clarion call, "come and enter the ark (Jesus)".

SKIN FOR SKIN

People say they can tell a lot about you by the people that you associate with. It is hard for our personalities and character traits not to rub off on others as we spend quality time in their presence. We are about to look at a Person of Interest who not only spent his time in the presence of a great man of God, but he was also an eye witness to the sovereignty of God and His power to work in those who have surrendered a pure heart for Him to love and work through. But a spirit of familiarity and entitlement will always be a potential thief and destroyer of what God could ultimately have for us. We can and will abuse the relationships we have with people, taking it and them for granted.

Elisha was the successor to Elijah the prophet of God. He had positioned himself to be present when God translated his servant, Elijah, swiftly from earth to heaven in a fiery chariot drawn by horses of fire. The older prophet had prophesied that if the younger were in place to see his translation to heaven, he would receive the double portion of the anointing on his life that he asked for. That is what happened. Elisha saw, received and accepted his master's "mantle" and the Bible records that he performed twice as many miracles as Elijah. As Elisha was a servant to a prophet, he also had a servant named Gehazi. As a servant to the men and women of God, one would be privy to the inside scoop of who God is and how he operates. There would probably be conversations about God and His dealings with man that no other person would hear or know about. Their master would have to trust the servant in order to allow them to serve. Our Master also will entrust us with His hidden secrets and treasures. Trust is the key. However, that trust can be abused and overstepped.

Naaman, the powerful Aramean commander was a leper. The dreaded and fatal disease presented itself as a death sentence on the commander. It was only after he reluctantly followed the instructions of the prophet Naaman, that he was healed. His gratitude came as an offer of silver and clothing as payment. But Elisha refused the offer and sent Naaman away. Gehazi, Elisha's servant saw this as an opportunity to be paid for his services, "My master was too easy on Naaman, this Aramean, by not accepting from him what he brought. As surely as the Lord lives, I will run after him and get something from him."(2 Kings 5:20 NIV). After all, hadn't he faithfully served Elisha for all these years? Was he not at his side attending to his every whim and heeding his every call? Therefore, when he caught up with Naaman who was on the road returning to his home, he made it seem as if his master had changed his mind and now needed the money and change of clothes, "Everything is all right," Gehazi answered. "My master sent me to say, 'Two young men from the company of the prophets have just come to me from the hill country of Ephraim. Please give them a talent of silver and two sets of clothing.' (2 Kings 5:22). Naaman was honored to oblige him and doubled the request sending him back to his master Elisha. Gehazi hid the items in his house before he went to stand before his master. When Elisha asked him where he had been, he lied and said nowhere. But what a prophet may not see with his physical eyes, God shows to his spiritual ones, "Was not my spirit with you when the man got down from his chariot to meet you? Is this the time to take money or to accept clothes" (5:26).

The hammer of judgment fell on Gehazi when Elisha cursed him with the same leprosy that had been upon Naaman. Oftentimes years of faithful service to and association with God's leaders or his people can lead us to deceitfully think that we are entitled to material benefits and privileges. Our line of thinking may be that we deserve to have what they have as if we are their equals. Sadly, not only Gehazi but also his descendants after him suffered the consequences of this KRAACKD POT'S lies, presumptions, envy, and spirit of familiarity.

HE LOVES ME, HE LOVES ME NOT

What happens when we find ourselves worrying about how people see us or are concerned about their approval and acceptance? And what do you do when you are in constant competition with a rival for the affections, approval, and attention of someone who only sees you as second best? Our Person of Interest had to make a decision about WHO loves her and who loves her not.

Jacob (whose name means "trickster"), the favored son of Rebekah, had to leave the home that he had always known, because of trickery and deception. The first deception was when he sold a pot of stew to his brother, Esau, in exchange for the coveted birthright that is destined for the firstborn son. Then he went along with the scheme of his mother, who favored him, to cheat Esau out of the blessing that was to be his upon the death of their father Isaac. Jacob received the blessing in his brother's place by his father Isaac but it was at the price of a death threat made towards him from Esau. So Jacob left his family on the run for his life.

The fugitive son ended up in the land of his mother's relatives where he fell in love with his cousin, Rachel. To Jacob's chagrin, the tables turned on him when the "trickster" became the tricked one. Laban, Rachel's father agreed to his offer to work seven years for the hand of his younger daughter, "So Jacob served seven years for Rachel, and they seemed *only* a few days to him because of the love he had for her" (Genesis 29:20). It was not until the morning after the wedding that the "deceiver" realized he had been deceived. Instead of Rachel, Laban had given the older and not as attractive daughter, Leah, to Jacob as a wife. Nevertheless, Jacob's love for Rachel, added another seven years of working for her father so that he could marry the woman of his dreams.

When God noticed that Jacob loved Rachel more than he loved Leah, he opened her womb and she began to bear Jacob children while Rachel was barren. The first child, Leah named, Reuben, meaning "misery". Surely, Jacob would love her now she thought. Her second son was named Simeon because she said the "Lord heard that I am not loved" (29:32). She became pregnant again with son number three who she named Levi, "Now, at last, my husband will become attached to me, because I have borne him three sons". The struggle of trying to win the approval and acceptance from man can be an endless and futile one. Man's love is based on conditions whereas God's is not. Jumping through hoops of approval can be tiring and leave the jumper feeling empty and rejected when the passion and desire is not reciprocated.

Finally, Leah bore a fourth son but this time her response was different. She realized that love, acceptance, and approval should come from One person alone, the One who loves us unconditionally, in spite and despite ourselves. We do not have to perform or prove anything to Him. Leah finally gave praise to the One Who loves her and was blessing her all the time, "This time I will praise the LORD." So she named him Judah" (v.35). BRKNVESSELS trust in God's UNFAILING and UNCONDITIONAL LOVE. There are no strings attached. And there is no room for competition because there is enough of God's love for all. The Bible says for God so loved the WORLD (John 3:3). This is the confidence and assurance that we have and can rest in for all of eternity.

A NEED TO KNOW BASIS

Suppose you were told to go to a house where a murderous and ruthless bounty hunter was residing. Not to mention that in doing so, you would be jeopardizing your own head. Later, you received news that the hunter would become as those he hunted and that he would turn many others lives around and over to his new Master and King. This Person of Interest found himself between a Rock and a very hard place. But the Rock won and the rest became history.

Saul of Tarsus was a very zealous, committed and passionate Pharisee (a keeper and upholder of the Jewish Mosaic law). He was a learned man, schooled and trained by Gamaliel, one of the greatest Pharisaic teachers of his day. It was this very zeal and passion of Saul that caused him to go on a mission. The mission? Destroy the new teaching called The Way, and everyone who claimed to be its followers. This "cult's" doctrines and way of life embraced its founder, a dead Jewish carpenter named Jesus whom people claimed was the Son of God, resurrected from the dead, and followed by hundreds. Stephen, a disciple of this new religion, was brought before the Sanhedrin and put on trial for preaching heresy and blasphemy by preaching in the forbidden name of Jesus. The religious leaders were so outraged and incensed at Stephen's accusations of murder against them and their blindness to the very law they were supposed to know, that they dragged him out of the city to stone him to death. A young Saul stood by watching over the clothes of Stephen's murderers as the stones they threw took the life of the first martyr of the Christian faith (Acts 7:57-58).

Years later, Saul got letters of permission from the high priest to search and seek out Christians in the synagogues of Damascus, where a great many believers were known to be. The letters gave him permission to torture, imprison and even kill those that he found in "The Way". On the road, a sudden light flashed into the eyes of the "bounty hunter", blinding him and knocking him off his horse. Falling to the ground, he heard the voice of the risen Christ, "Saul, Saul, why are you persecuting Me?" Jesus identified who he was and Saul asked the question that we all must ask when we are called by the Lord, "Lord, what do You want me to do?" (Acts 9:3-6). He was told to go into the city where he would receive further instructions. Led as a blind man by the soldiers who were with him, he was three days without sight, neither eating nor drinking anything.

Ananias, a devout disciple of Jesus received a vision from Him. In it, he was told, "Arise and go to the street called Straight, and inquire at the house of Judas for one called Saul of Tarsus, for behold, he is praying. And in a vision he has seen a man named Ananias coming in and putting his hand on him, so that he might receive his sight"(Acts 9:11-12). The terrified response from Ananias reminded God of who this person was and what his horrific actions had been towards God's people. He had heard that he was on his way to Damascus to wreak further havoc on the church there, "Lord, I have heard from many about this man, how much harm he has done to Your saints in Jerusalem. And here he has authority from the chief priests to bind all who call on Your name" (Acts 9:13-14). How could this be? Questions had to have begun to swirl in Ananias's head. How can God ask me to risk my life and do something like this? Does He know what could happen to me if I go through with this? The answer is "yes", He knows. However, His plan and His ways of doing things are greater than we can ever think or imagine. One thing that is certain about Him, He will never ask us to do anything we cannot. And He will give us all that we need (strength and courage in this case) to get it done. God has plans that we know not of and He will use whomever He chooses to accomplish them, "But the Lord said to him, "Go, for he is a chosen vessel of Mine to bear My name before Gentiles, kings, and the children of Israel. For I will show him how many things he must suffer for My name's sake" (Acts 9:15-16).

It was at this same time that God also showed Saul Ananias coming to him. And when he did arrive, he placed his hand on Saul and said, " Brother Saul, the Lord Jesus, who appeared to you on the road as you came, has sent me that you may receive your sight and be filled with the Holy Spirit" (9:17). Something like scales fell off Saul's eyes and he was able to see. He spent several days in Damascus, preaching the word of God immediately. To the surprise, doubt and questions of the believers there, he grew stronger in spite of it. Moreover, his fellow Jews who had a conspiracy to kill him threatened even his own life but he escaped from their hands.

If it had not been for a BRKNVESSEL, who surrendered to and trusted the plan of God, we would not have two-thirds of the New Testament written by one of the greatest apostles that ever lived. We would not have the epistles that he wrote as inspired words of the Holy Spirit Who taught him, giving him the sustenance of a Christian's way of living and believing. Everything that God told Ananias would happen to Paul was fulfilled in Paul's' life. Ananias is a perfect example of what God can and will do through us when we lean not to our own understanding but totally and completely trust and obey Him in all our ways! (Proverbs 3:5)

NOT FOR SALE

These days it seems like if you have the right amount of money you can pretty much buy anything. A man had an old vintage car sitting in his yard. The car was a classic and worth a lot of money. The man knew this and was reminded every week as someone would drive by his house and stop to ring his doorbell. They would inquire about the car and offer to buy it from him. Regardless of the amount of money offered, the man would always decline and refuse the offer. After several months of these episodes, he finally put a sign on the car-NOT FOR SALE! Our Person of Interest found out that everything has a price but some things are NOT FOR SALE.

After the death of Christendom's first martyr, Stephen, the early church began to suffer much persecution from the status quo religious leaders and the reigning emperors of Rome. It was during this time that Saul arose (before his conversion and name change to Apostle Paul) wreaking havoc on the church," But Saul began to destroy the church. Going from house to house, he dragged off men and women and put them in prison." (Acts 8:3), having been given permission to do so by the high priests of the

Jewish synagogue. As horrific as persecutions were, they proved to be a part of the plan of a Sovereign God. The newly converted "Christians" scattered and fled for their lives spreading the gospel wherever they went. It has been said that the early church was birthed out of and grew from the bloody seeds of those who gave up their lives to bring life to others through the message of the risen Savior, Lord and King, Jesus!

Philip, an evangelist went to the city of Samaria. In the city, there was a man named Simon who for many years practiced sorcery and with his deeds and words persuaded the people to believe in him, "and all the people, from the least to the greatest, heeded his words and said, "This man is the divine power called the Great Power." They paid close attention to him because he had amazed them for a long time with his sorcery" (Acts 8:10). But when the people heard the gospel preached by Philip, they believed and were baptized. The true word of God is sharper than any two-edged sword. It has the power to change hearts, minds, and lives. Anything that Satan tries to fabricate, pales in comparison and will always only be a cheap counterfeit! Simon also heard the preached word, believed and was baptized. From that point on, he followed Philip closely, observing the power of God operating through his life (signs and wonders will always follow an evangelist). When the apostles Peter and John were sent from Jerusalem to Samaria to lay hands on and pray for the people to receive the gift of the Holy Spirit, many did. As Simon saw this power, he offered the men money, "Give me this power as well," he said, "so that everyone on whom I lay my hands may receive the Holy

Spirit" (Acts 8:19). But his offer was refused as well as the motive behind his request, "But Peter said to him, "Your money perish with you, because you thought that the gift of God could be purchased with money! You have neither part nor portion in this matter, for your heart is not right in the sight of God. Repent therefore of this your wickedness, and pray God if perhaps the thought of your heart may be forgiven you. For I see that you are poisoned by bitterness and bound by iniquity." (8:20-23). Through the discerning of spirit and word of knowledge (1 Corinthians 12:8-11), Peter was able to expose what was really going on behind the scene. The Holy Spirit came to give us power to be witnesses of Christ (Acts 1:8). He also empowers us to live and walk the Christian life victoriously. Only a heart that is pure and humble will understand that His gifts and power is not something that we can buy, earn or use for our own benefits or personal gain.

Simon saw a power greater than what he had operated in. He was able to say some words and put up a pretense in order to get close to who he thought the power source was (Peter). His heart was not pure and nor was his motives of selfishness, greed and personal gain. He neither cared about making a difference in the lives of people or in honoring and magnifying God. He was a KRAACKD POT that had a form of godliness but denied the very power of God. Lesson learned for him and for us, GOD IS NOT FOR SALE!

A MAN FOR ALL SEASONS

Our year is divided into four climatic changes, spring, summer, autumn, and winter. Each division has its own weather patterns and daylight hours that depend on the earth's changing position to the sun. There are also seasons throughout life, age, marital status, careers, economic status, and physical health and wellbeing. Our Person of Interest went through several "seasons" in his life. But unlike the seasons of the year that change based on the sun, he stayed the same based on his faith in God.

After triumphantly exiting Egypt by the powerful hand of God, the children of Israel stood in the Wilderness of Paran waiting to hear what they were to do next. God instructed Moses to choose a leader from each tribe to go on a mission to spy out the land He had promised them. Moses chose a leader from each of the twelve tribes to go. Forty days later, they returned to report to their leader what they saw. They gave Moses this account: "We went into the land to which you sent us, and it does flow with milk and honey! Here is its fruit. But the people who live there are powerful, and the cities are fortified and very large. We even saw descendants of Anak there. (Numbers 13:27-28 NIV). The response of the leaders was one of hesitation and fear, despite the fact that God had already promised the land to them. God would not ask us to do something that we could not do. Whatever we may lack, He will provide, as He is known as "Jehovah Jireh", the God that sees ahead and provides. But Caleb, who was 40 years old at the time, had a different set of eyes, ears and a different heart than the majority. He chose to see things with the eyes of the spirit and with a heart of courage that comes from trusting God, "Then Caleb silenced the people before Moses and said, "We should go up and take possession of the land, for we can certainly do it" (Numbers 13:30). Either we can say what we feel or we can say what God says. The rest of the leaders were controlled by what they saw and felt, FEAR, DOUBT, and UNBELIEF. Their "fearful" reports put fear in the hearts of the rest of the people who immediately complained and cried out against Moses and Aaron. They began to regret that they had ever left Egypt, even though it was God who brought them out. And they entertained the thought of returning back to the place of bondage. This outright rebellion against, God caused Moses and Aaron to tear their clothes and fall to their knees in repentance. Joshua and Caleb also tore their clothes, pleading with the children of Israel NOT to rebel against God, "Only do not rebel against the Lord. And do not be afraid of the people of the land, because we will devour them. Their protection is gone, but the Lord is with us. Do not be afraid of them" (Numbers 14:9). Instead of encouraged hearts ready to obey God and take what He gave them, Joshua and Caleb's pleas were met with death threats of stoning.

The situation was more than God could stand. He intervened with a pronouncement of judgment against the children of Israel. For 40 years they would wander in the wilderness, a year for every day that the spies were gone, "So tell them, 'As surely as I live, declares the Lord, I will do to you the very thing I heard you say: In this wilderness your bodies will fall—every one of you twenty years old or more who was counted in the census and who has grumbled against me. Not one of you will enter the land I swore with uplifted hand to make your home, except Caleb son of Jephunneh and Joshua son of Nun" (Joshua 14:28-30). For forty years, corpses fell in the desert, family members died and others were born taking their place. Nevertheless, it was only Joshua and Caleb, now 85 years old, who got to see what God had promised.

After the death of Moses, Joshua became the leader who took the children into the Promised Land. As the land was conquered, it was divided up and given to certain people. Caleb, though 85 years of age, was not to be denied, "Now the people of Judah approached Joshua at Gilgal, and Caleb son of Jephunneh the Kenizzite said to him, "You know what the Lord said to Moses the man of God at Kadesh Barnea about you and me. I was forty years old when Moses the servant of the Lord sent me from Kadesh Barnea to explore the land. And I brought him back a report according to my convictions, but my fellow Israelites who went up with me made the hearts of the people melt in fear. I, however, followed the Lord my God wholeheartedly. So on that day Moses swore to me, 'The land on which your feet have walked will be your inheritance and that of your children forever, because you have followed the Lord my God wholeheartedly. "Now then, just as the Lord promised, he has kept me alive for forty-five years since the time he said this to Moses, while Israel moved about in the wilderness. So here I am today, eighty-five years old! I am still as strong today as the day Moses sent me out; I'm just as vigorous to go out to battle now as I was then. Now give me this hill country that the Lord promised me that day" (Joshua 14:6-12)

Caleb went through the seasons of seeing the faithful hand of God move on behalf of His people. He saw people he knew and loved, fall dead in the desert because of their unbelief. He wandered for forty years for something that he was not responsible for. When he came to the place of promise, his response was not one of doubt, bitterness, or weariness. He was just as secure in God's promise and faithfully trusted Him just as he did in the earlier seasons of his life. There will be the dryness of fall, the death and cold of winter, the renewal of spring and the lush greenery and warmth of the summer. A BRKNVESSEL will go through the changing, topsy-turvy, roller-coaster seasons of life and remain HOPEFUL and TRUSTFUL. Filled with EXPECTATION, they will anticipate the fulfillment of God's promises, which are YES, and AMEN!

BIG I'S AND LITTLE YOU'S

Hollywood over the years has depicted many "rags to riches stories". The plot usually goes like this; a person comes from nothing, is going nowhere with nobody. Then there is a change of circumstances and turn of events that moves them to some place, going somewhere with somebody. Our last Person of Interest went in the opposite direction. Their claim to fame was that they went from "riches to rags", as they attempted to climb the ladder to become a Big "I" to little "You" (and me).

If you were to ask someone to describe the devil, they would probably use words like, "red suit, pitch-fork, horns, and a tail". At least that is the visual usually displayed. However, that is not how scripture shows him. In Ezekiel 28, there is a proclamation against the prince of Tyre from God through the prophet, "Son of man, say to the prince of Tyre, 'Thus says the Lord God: 'Because your heart is lifted up, And you say, 'I am a god, I sit in the seat of gods, In the midst of the seas,' Yet you are a man, and not a god, Though you set your heart as the heart of a god" (Ezekiel 28:1-2). Evidently, the man saw himself as a god and therefore equal to if not greater than the One who made him. His speech, decisions, and behavior were all characteristic of one who is walking in PRIDE.

The tide changes when a proclamation is then directed to the "king of Tyre" in verse 11. What follows is a "behind the scenes" account of a being that obviously was not a human. He was full of wisdom and perfect in beauty, present in the Garden of Eden and covered with precious gemstones. Musical instruments were prepared for him on the day he was created and made a part of him. He resided on the mountain of God and was chosen, anointed and established by God to be the angelic cherub that stood guard over the Almighty's throne. He was perfect in all his ways until iniquity was found in him (Ezekiel 28:14-17) And what was the iniquity? The prophet Isaiah sheds light on this in chapter fourteen of his book. In verse twelve, we clearly read about the fall of Satan, whose name was Lucifer prior to. PRIDE caused him to make five "I will" statements, "You said in your heart, "I will ascend to the heavens; I will raise my throne above the stars of God; I will sit enthroned on the mount of assembly, on the utmost heights of Mount Zaphon. I will ascend above the tops of the clouds; I will make myself like the Most High." But you are brought down to the realm of the dead, to the depths of the pit. (Isaia 14:13-14). Each statement showed the fatal symptoms of pride, arrogance, presumption, boasting, conceit, high-mindedness, and haughtiness. The first thing to note is that when we are full of pride, there will be warning signs that will point right back to us. The first one is, we will always refer to the personal pronoun "I" (I will, I do, I am, etc). Instead of the credit and the glory going to God, we will point back to ourselves (the Big "I").

God tells us that His glory will not go to any man, woman, boy or girl, "I am the LORD; that is my name! I will not yield my glory to another or my praise to idols" (Isaiah 42:8).

The second issue and warning sign of a Big "I" is an attitude of unwarranted entitlement, confidence, and ambition. We will no longer be grateful or satisfied with where God has placed us. Instead we will try to usurp or supplant others and even God Himself (Genesis 11:1-9)). It is unwise and detrimental to our spiritual well-being to forget that it is the Lord who chooses, anoints, gives spiritual gifts and promotes us to where He desires. Satan's (whose name means "deceiver") beginning was a "rich" one but pride and arrogance reduced this fallen angel's (Luke 10:18) position to that of man's mortal enemy (and therefore God's). He is the father of lies and the diabolical deceiver of humankind. To the glory of God, he is also a defeated foe through and by the blood of the Lamb of God and risen King of kings and Lord of lords. This KRAACKD POT who had a beginning as a BRKNVESSEL has an ending of eternal destruction and defeat (Revelation 20:7-10). His demise is a constant reminder that "pride goes before destruction and a haughty spirit before a fall" (Proverbs 16:18).

ABOUT RENE'

Rene' Marie Jones is a dynamic Praise & Worship Leader, a passionate and propelling Bible teacher, the founder of Mount Zion Christian Church-Rocky Mount, North Carolina Agape' Women's Fellowship, and founder & CEO of WINGSPAN, INC., a nonprofit organization that educates, empowers and encourages a community through its various outreach programs. She is a licensed workshop instructor and presenter of **The Look of the Leader**, a leadership workshop that dynamically prepares people to lead with a servant's heart and to make an impact on the world they influence.

Rene' has traveled to the continent of Africa and the country of Jamaica where she has taught and presented workshops on Christian Education and Biblical Leadership. It is to these places that she and her husband, Pastor Garland W. Jones, serve as "Kingdom Ambassadors". She has an endearing love for the people of God and is deeply concerned about their spiritual growth, development, and maturity. As a servant of God, who is intimately involved with Him, Rene' desires to help prepare His body for the work of the ministry and to draw the people of God into a more intimate and personal walk with the Master.

Connect with Rene' on

TWITTER
https://twitter.com/naejnz

FACEBOOK
https://www.facebook.com/brknvessels/

INSTAGRAM
https://www.instagram.com/brknvessels/

WEBSITE
https://renemariejones.com/

www.ingramcontent.com/pod-product-compliance
Lightning Source LLC
Chambersburg PA
CBHW021406290426
44108CB00010B/415